God's
Instruction
BOOK

FOUNDATIONAL TRUTHS
OF PROVERBS

BY
GARY L. GIBSON

God's Instruction Book

Trilogy Christian Publishers A Wholly Owned Subsidiary of Trinity Broadcasting Network

2442 Michelle Drive Tustin, CA 92780

Manufactured in the United States of America

10 9 8 7 6 5 4 3 2 1

Library of Congress Cataloging-in-Publication Data is available.

ISBN: 979-8-88738-326-2

E-ISBN: 979-8-88738-327-9

Dedication

To all those who do not yet know the forgiveness of Jesus Christ and the power of the Holy Spirit to transform lives into holy, acceptable men and women for the glory of God the Father.

Table of Contents

Prologue

Exodus 20:12 (TLB), "Honor your father and mother, that you may have a long, good life in the land the Lord your God will give you."

Proverbs 1:7 (TLB), "How does a man become wise? The first step is to trust and reverence the Lord."

Proverbs 1:23 (TLB), "Come here and listen to me! I'll pour out the spirit of wisdom upon you and make you wise."

Proverbs 3:4–5 (TLB), "If you want favor with both God and man, and a reputation for good judgment and common sense, then trust the Lord completely; don't ever trust yourself."

Proverbs 3:21 (TLB), "Have two goals; wisdom—that is, knowing and doing right—and common sense. Don't let them slip away."

Proverbs 4:7, "Determination to be wise is the first step toward becoming wise!"

Proverbs 3:16–17 (TLB), "Wisdom gives: a long, good life, riches, honor, pleasure, peace."

Proverbs 19:27 (TLB), "Stop listening to teaching that contradicts what you know is right."

I call heaven and earth to witness against you
that today I have set before you life or death,

7

blessing or curse. Oh, that you would choose life; that you and your children might live! Choose to love the Lord your God and to obey him and to cling to him, for he is your life and the length of your days.

Deuteronomy 30:19–20 (TLB)

Chapter 1:
A Confession of Faith

We often hear that people believe in God. Over eighty percent of all Americans say they believe in God. Just how difficult is that? We should be able to see God all around us if we have our eyes open. God exists in everything we are able to see, whether it is with the naked eye, through a telescope, or through a microscope. His signature is throughout His creation.

Certainly, the Hubbell Telescope has broadened our vision of the vast expanse of our universe. What we *cannot* see with our naked eye becomes more magnificent than the things we *can* see. Looking through a microscope allows us to see the intricate structure of cells and the unique manner in which each is adapted to a bodily or plant function. God's signature is one of wisdom, knowledge, and understanding. Because it is, there are those who will worship the stars, the moon, the earth, and even wooden sticks and continue to say that they believe in God. This brings me to the first truth.

God is. God is infinite. He always was, and He always will be God. God is three persons; God the Father, Jesus Christ, His only begotten Son, and God the Holy Spirit.

We speak of God as the Godhead—three persons in one, or God the holy trinity.

It is difficult to understand with finite minds that God can be all three—and that all three can be as one God. God is Alpha and Omega. Before there was anything, God was. And at the end of time or the end of the age, God is. In Exodus 3:14, God referred to himself as "I am" when Moses asked, "Whom should I say sent me?" Before the earth, universe, or time existed, God the holy trinity was there. John 1:1–3 (TLB) states, "Before anything else existed, there was Christ, with God. He has always been alive and is himself God. He created everything there is—nothing exists that he didn't make." This established Christ as the creator of our world and all things in the world—including man.

Faith Confession

I believe in God.

I believe in God's Word.

I believe in God's Son, Jesus Christ.

I believe in creation because it is described in God's Word.

I believe that God created the heavens and the earth.

I believe that Jesus Christ is the only begotten Son of God.

I believe that Jesus Christ died on the cross for my sins.

I believe that I was chosen to be a follower of Jesus Christ.

I believe in the holy trinity, God the Father, Jesus Christ, and the Holy Spirit.

I believe the Holy Spirit dwells within me.

I believe in life after death.

I believe there is a heaven and hell.

I believe that Jesus Christ is coming again to dwell over a literal kingdom.

I believe that my salvation was secured on the day of Christ's crucifixion.

Chapter 2:
Creation

God created the earth and inhabited it with man, plants, animals, and every living thing. There are numerous theories as to how the earth and man came into existence.

Each theory of man presents bizarre findings, which often are based on erroneous assumptions and are not supported by factual evidence. Such is the theory of evolution.

According to the evolution theory, man evolved over billions of years, and yet there is no evidence of such a transition in plants or animals. Such assumptions are based on information at hand at a given point in time, along with an overactive imagination. Once this idea was presented and accepted as a plausible theory, it became necessary to defend it as "truth." The same can be said for "the Big Bang theory," or the idea that we were visited and inhabited by aliens from a distant galaxy.

Ideas such as this beg for answers to the questions of where did "they" come from and how did "they" begin life? If man is an evolved higher form of life, how is it possible that larger complex forms of life, such as the dinosaur, existed millions of years before man? And where did they come from?

Proverbs 13:19 (TLB) says, "It is pleasant to see plans develop. That is why fools refuse to give them up even when they are wrong." We can see a plan developing in our country and in all parts of the world today. We live in a pluralistic society where teachers find it necessary to present various theories of men in our school systems. However, we are prohibited from presenting God's Word as a possible alternative. The plan would appear to be the discarding of the Word of God as heresy in order to elevate man's theories to a more acceptable level.

An obvious tactic of the minority population of atheistic thinkers is to remove the truth from consideration. How is it possible that such a small minority of our population can dictate and indoctrinate our children, forcing them to choose between two or three theories of how life began? These are theories that have not withstood the scrutiny of time and exclude God's written Word (truth). What we ultimately accomplish by this is to substitute man's ideas in place of God's Word. Without realizing it, we are succeeding in joining forces with Satan, who knows that God's Word must be totally removed in order to deceive mankind.

It is not possible for us to understand with our finite minds the wisdom of God. We understand gravity when something falls on our heads or discover the effects of electricity when lightning illuminates the sky. Understanding how God could design a universe where the earth rotates in space, spinning like a top as it orbits around the sun, becomes a bit more challenging to our minds.

The earth spins at approximately 1,000 miles per hour, and yet the earth's gravitational pull, in our atmospheric density, prevents us from being thrown through space. The earth's rotation gives us twenty-four hours a day. The moon rotates around the earth and gives us our tides. The earth's axis of rotation is tilted at an angle of 23.5 degrees, which gives us our climate changes. The earth makes a full rotation around the sun every 365.25 days.

We can measure a mean solar day and discover that it consists of 86,400 mean solar seconds (sl). There are minor fluctuations measured in 0–5 milliseconds (ms). The consistency of God's creation is designed according to His wisdom. It is absolute and sovereign.

Animals breathe in oxygen from the air and exhale carbon dioxide. Plants take in carbon dioxide and give off oxygen in a process called photosynthesis. Water is essential for plant and animal life and is constantly replenished as it passes through various forms of vapor—solid and liquid. The fact that we drink water daily and use it to water our fields does not diminish the volume that God placed on

Earth. Our atmosphere allows both plants and animals to exist in a delicate balance of pressure, gases, and temperature. All of the above occurs with such consistency that it can be measured with fine instruments over thousands of years.

Our entire universe is set in similar systematic motion with millions upon billions of stars. How was this accomplished? Only by an Almighty God who could but speak His Word and physical planets, stars, our sun, and the visible universe came into being. How is it possible that all of this was done with such accuracy and precision in the absence of expendable energy and waste? All of the above is in need of one additional element to sustain life, and that element is light—which will be discussed in the next chapter.

The magnetic forces and gravitational attractions of the planets, moon, and stars in our own universe would collapse and implode on themselves were it not for the design and wisdom of God. Yet, we teach our children that this all happened by chance or that aliens visited us from a distant planet. Are we so desperate to deny God that we would propose such an absurd hypothesis and defend it as truth?

Ecclesiastes 10:12–13 (TLB), "It is pleasant to listen to

wise words, but a fool's speech brings him to ruin. Since he begins with a foolish premise, his conclusion is sheer madness."

Chapter 3:
God Created Light and
Is the Light

On the first day of creation, God said,

> "Let there be light." And light appeared [at
> 186,000 miles per second]. And God was
> pleased with it and divided the light from the
> darkness. [So He let it shine for a while, and
> then there was darkness again.] He called
> the light "daytime," and the darkness "night-
> time." Together they formed the first day.
>
> **Genesis 1:3–5 (TLB)**

It is of interest to note that the sun, the moon, and the
stars were not created until the fourth day (Genesis 1:14–
19). We tend to think that the sun, moon, and stars are our
source of light, and they obviously are. But without Christ,
light ceases to exist. This is both a metaphor and a reality.
Hell can even be imagined as the absence of Christ and the
absence of light. John 1:4–5 (TLB) says, "Eternal life is in
him [Christ], and this life gives light to all mankind. His
life is the light that shines through the darkness—and the

darkness can never extinguish it."

We have been able to reproduce light through the development of electricity. We are learning some of its properties and how to transmit it over vast distances. The production of electricity has made it possible to produce goods, have transportation, illuminate our homes, and provide conveniences such as heating and air conditioning.

The availability of electricity is a major factor that helps us to distinguish the difference between a developing country and a third-world country. Even with the development of the laser, our understanding of the principles of light and its possible uses is in its infancy. Albert Einstein published the theory of the laser in 1917. It was not until May 16, 1960, some forty-three years later, that an American scientist developed the first laser.

We've learned how to take a substance (fuel) and change its properties in order to produce energy, which can be converted into light (with substantial waste).

You may have heard recent comments about how you can "save electricity." The fact is, you cannot save electricity that is not consumed apart from a secondary storage source such as a battery. Generators operate at a constant speed and produce a constant flow of electricity which is either consumed or dissipated. If electric usage were suddenly to be reduced to twenty percent (20%) instead of eighty percent (80%), the electrical supply company would, out of necessity, have to increase their rates by four times or shift the electricity to another power grid.

You can reduce your electrical consumption, which could result in potential individual savings. The greatest savings occurs when the generated electrical power can be shifted to additional users by means of a power grid.

Electricity was not invented; it was discovered. The wisdom of God placed it there at creation along with other "inventions" yet to be discovered. When Solomon said, "There is nothing new under the sun" (Ecclesiastes 1:9, NIV), he knew that God, by design, created many things that man, over time, would discover.

Chapter 4:
God Created Man

God created man from the dust of the earth and breathed into it the breath of life. Genesis 2:7 (TLB) states, "The time came when the Lord God formed a man's body from the dust of the ground and breathed into it the breath of life. And man became a person." Thousands of years after this account, we are able to analyze the physical properties of man and find that he was made from the dust of the earth.

God created man and woman not as children but as adults of childbearing age. God caused a sleep to come upon Adam, and He took a rib from Adam and made him a helpmate called Eve. Adam called her "woman" since she was a part of his physical body. It has been argued incorrectly that man has one less rib than a woman because God removed one of Adam's ribs. Man actually has the same number of ribs as a woman. If a doctor were to remove one of your ribs, do you think your offspring would be born with one less rib? It was not necessary for God to create Eve as a baby. God made her a mature woman and helpmate to Adam of childbearing age.

Scientists have looked at rocks and the earth's structure and estimated that it is millions of years old. Is it possible that God created the earth to *appear* to be millions of years old? Would that be too difficult a task for God to accomplish? Or would that simply be too difficult a task for man to comprehend? Yet some find it easier to believe that an alien established life on Earth.

God planted a garden in Eden with a variety of trees that produced the choicest of fruit. Again we see that God made *mature* trees, which produced fruit. In this garden, He placed two trees at the center. The first was "the tree of life," and the second was "the tree of conscience," which gave man the knowledge of *good and evil*. Genesis 2:16–17 (TLB) states,

> But the Lord God gave the man this warn-
> ing: "You may eat any fruit in the garden
> except fruit from the Tree of Conscience—
> for its fruit will open your eyes to make you
> aware of right and wrong, good and bad. If
> you eat its fruit, you will be doomed to die."

Now the serpent (Satan) appeared to the woman Eve and convinced her that she could eat the forbidden fruit from the "tree of conscience" and not die. Satan's real lie was that Adam and Eve had the *right* to choose to do what God had told them *not* to do. Satan's next lie was that Adam and Eve would be like God. Eve's eyes would be open, and she would be able to distinguish between good and evil. She ate some of the fruit and gave some to her husband, Adam, and he ate. They became aware that they were naked. Adam and Eve saw for the very first time that they were naked and hid from God. Did Adam and Eve see their nakedness as sin or the potential for sin for the very first time because they disobeyed God?

As a result of Adam and Eve's disobedience, God said a curse was on the soil, and Adam and all mankind would sweat to master it until his dying day. Eve's curse was that women would bear children with much pain. Satan's third lie was that Adam and Eve would surely not die. Adam and Eve did die, and they returned to the soil from which they were made.

God banished Adam and Eve from the garden and placed angels at its entrance in order that they would not eat from the "tree of life."

Chapter 5:
Adam's Sin—
Christ's Redemption

By one man's (Adam) disobedience to God, sin came to all mankind. By one man's (Jesus Christ) sacrifice, forgiveness would freely be given to all who would believe in the Lord Jesus Christ.

You might find it difficult to understand why Eve and then Adam would eat from the only tree in the garden that God said they could not eat. Would they have lived forever if they had eaten from the "tree of life"? That is a thought-provoking question. We are presented with the same question as our personal choice. Which tree will we eat from? Here are some questions we each must answer.

1. Are we convinced by the persuasive words of Satan, who tells us we can be like God and make our own decisions?

2. Do you think right (fair) or wrong varies according to our individual circumstances or understanding?

3. Are you wise enough to reject *the* "lies of Satan" because you consider yourself to be a good person?

4. Do you believe that fairness should take priority over God's Law?

5. Are you smart enough to recognize that which is evil?

6. Are you resisting the temptation to do something wrong simply because you fear you might be caught?

7. Is your definition of evil "that which I would never do" or "the line I would never cross"?

8. Would you tell a lie in order to save your job or make a sale if it would not hurt another person?

9. Do you think that tolerance of another's beliefs requires us not to call something sin if the other person thinks it is okay?

Each of us has come from a totally different background. What if you came from a poor family with a drunken, abusive father? Or maybe there was not a father in the home at all, and you had to resort to stealing food so that you didn't starve. Some of us can't imagine what it would be like to be raised in a family where drug use is a common daily event or where you learned to steal at a very young age to support your parent's drug habit.

What if you did not have parents and were moved from house to house and subjected to abuse by older adults or foster parents? Should it be the government's responsibility to make sure that a child grows up in a safe environment with equal rights and opportunities? Should children from dysfunctional families be treated as victims or criminals when they break the law?

We can all see the influence of circumstances when deciding what is wrong or evil, legal or illegal, and how punishment might vary. However, I am certain that defining "good" will be easier to understand. For instance, would you agree that being poor is unfair and it's the government's responsibility to eliminate the poor by providing whatever food and money are necessary for them to live a similar lifestyle as you and I enjoy?

What are some of the good things we could agree on that would make life fairer? Should we provide free abortions to women who are likely to give birth to a deformed baby? How about free college education and healthcare for everyone? We could ensure that everyone has a livable minimum wage. If there were no jobs where they lived, we could just send them money every month to live on. Should we rely on the government or our court system to determine for us what is right (fair) and what is wrong?

You can see by the above illustration that "good and evil" are Satan's attempts to distort God's truth. Our humanistic desire is to be like God by showing more "fairness" than God shows. Man tends to look at concepts of good, fair, greater good, rights, tolerance, and social justice as being superior to God's plan. God simply asks us to accept Him by faith and trust Him to teach us wisdom, common sense, and understanding through reading His Word.

We see in the Bible in the Old Testament that because the children of Israel did not have a king, "For in those days Israel had no king, so everyone did whatever he wanted to—whatever seemed right [fair] in his own eyes" (Judges 17:6, TLB). This is a strong indication that many of us either want to be told what to do or to have the freedom to decide for ourselves what is right. In instances where a king was given the responsibility to tell the people what to think and how to believe, there was corruption and often destruction because the kings were idol worshipers or oppressors of their people. Entire countries were destroyed because "the king did what was right in his own eyes" rather than being obedient to God's instruction.

Just how much influence do others have over our decisions? Truly we were born into a sinful world with corruption, inequities, and greed. The entire world appears intent on inculcating us with every evil thought. After all, do we not have the "right to know"? Each new invention or discovery is yet another opportunity to bring evil thoughts and images into our lives—via movies, television, and the internet. This gives us the opportunity to see "good or evil" in order to determine which we will choose. If you choose "good" over "evil," you may believe you have made the better choice. In fact, you think you *have* made the "right" choice.

Herein is the real problem. We believe the choice is choosing "good" over "evil." That is not the choice. That is the "lie." The real choice is between obedience to God's Word or believing Satan's lie that we have the *right* to choose between "good and evil." We face the same choices that Eve and Adam faced in the Garden of Eden.

All that is wrong with the world today stems from man's disobedience to God. Each of us must make our own decision to follow the way which is broad and easy or to go down the path through the narrow gate. The narrow gate is Jesus Christ, the "tree of life," who was crucified on a tree to pay the price for our sins, making us acceptable for eternal life with Him in heaven. John 3:16 (TLB) says, "For God loved the world so much that he gave his only Son so that anyone who believes in him shall not perish but have eternal life."

It was God's plan from the beginning for Christ not only to be the creator but the only sacrifice worthy to redeem man and forgive his sins.

Jesus said in Matthew 11:25–27 (NIV),

> I praise you, Father, Lord of heaven and
> earth, because you have hidden these things
> from the wise and learned, and revealed
> them to little children. Yes, Father, for this

was what you were pleased to do. All things
have been committed to me by my Father.
No one knows the Son except the Father,
and no one knows the Father except the Son
and those to whom the Son chooses to reveal
him.

Paul states in 1 Corinthians 1:27 (NIV), "But God chose the foolish things of the world to shame the wise; God chose the weak things of the world to shame the strong."

Chapter 6:
Believe God's Word—
Reject "Satan's Lies"

"Satan's lie" in the Garden of Eden was that Eve had the "right" to choose between "good and evil." He tempted Eve with the claim that she could be like God and denied God's warning to Adam that if he ate the fruit, he would die. Satan is the deceiver, and the truth is not in him. He called God the liar when he told Eve that surely they would not die if they ate the fruit. Satan did not have the power or authority to make Adam and Eve like God. Satan was not a creator of anything except deceit and lies. Satan, therefore, could not provide Adam the choice of "good" because only God is good. Satan cannot give you what he doesn't have the power to give.

God gave each of us the free will to choose, just like Adam and Eve. The choice we have to make is between "God's truth" and "Satan's lie." If we believe that we are intelligent or wise enough to determine for ourselves what is right, good, or fair in the absence of God's Word, then we, like Adam, have been deceived by "Satan's lie."

Recorded in the book of Luke, we can read the account of Satan tempting Christ in the wilderness (desert) for forty days. In Luke 4:3 (TLB), Satan said, "If you are God's Son, tell this stone to become a loaf of bread." First of all, Satan knew that Christ was the Son of God. He had just spent forty days in the wilderness tempting Jesus and had known His deity from the time he (Satan) was created.

Every evil spirit that Christ cast out of man was able to instantly identify that Christ was the Messiah, the Son of God. Although Christ was very hungry, He was not going to obey Satan by turning a stone into a loaf of bread! What harm would it have been for Christ to turn the stone into a loaf of bread? If Christ was very hungry, wasn't this justified? Did Christ have the power and authority to perform such a miracle? Satan surely knew that He did.

Jesus' response to Satan was to quote God's Word. Luke 4:4, "But Jesus replied, 'It is written in the Scriptures, "Other things in life are much more important than bread!" '" Jesus was quoting from Deuteronomy 8:3 (KJV), "That man doth not live by bread only, but by every word that proceedeth out of the mouth of the Lord doth man live."

"Then Satan took him up and showed him all the kingdoms of the world in a moment of time" (Luke 4:5, TLB). Satan said, "I will give you all these splendid kingdoms and their glory—for they are mine to give to anyone I wish—if you will only ...worship me" (Luke 4:6–7, TLB). Christ replied to "Satan's lie" with, "We must worship God, and him alone. So it is written in the scriptures" (Luke 4:8, TLB). Verses 9–12 (TLB),

> Then Satan took him to Jerusalem to a high
> roof of the Temple and said, "If you are the
> Son of God, jump off! For the Scriptures say
> that God will send his angels to guard you
> and to keep you from crashing to the pave-
> ment below!" Jesus replied, "The Scriptures
> also say, 'Do not put the Lord your God to a
> foolish test.'"

Satan resorted to quoting Scripture in order to support his "lie." Jesus, in this context, identified Himself to Satan as "the Lord your God." Christ, because He was God, chose the Word of God as truth over His "right" to choose between "good and evil."

Chapter 7:
The Law

God gave Moses the ten commandments for the children of Israel and thereby established God's laws for man. The ten commandments were given to Moses and the children of Israel for the explicit purpose of showing that man was not capable of keeping God's Law. God knew that man would not, and could not, be good enough to be acceptable for eternal life in heaven. Because of this, Christ had to be the blood sacrifice for sin in order to make us (man) acceptable for eternal life with Him.

The Ten Commandments
- Thou shall have no other gods before Me.
- Thou shall not make for yourself a carved image or any likeness of anything that is in heaven above, or that is in the earth beneath, or that is in the water under the earth. For I, the Lord, am a jealous God, visiting the iniquity of the fathers upon the children unto the third and fourth generation of them that hate me.
- You shall not take the name of the Lord your God in vain.

- Remember the Sabbath day to keep it holy.
- Honor your father and your mother. That you may have a long, good life in the land the Lord your God will give you.
- Thou shall not murder.
- Thou shall not commit adultery.
- Thou shall not steal.
- Thou shall not bear false witness against your neighbor. (You must not lie.)
- You shall not covet your neighbor's house; thou shall not covet your neighbor's wife, nor his male servant, nor his female servant, nor his ox, nor his donkey, nor anything that is your neighbor's.

The ten commandments are the framework of all God's laws. When we depart from these laws, we allow man's thinking to supersede "God's truth," and destruction and chaos are inevitable. When Christ came, He did not eliminate the Law; He perfected the Law by His act of mercy. God's Law, contained in the ten commandments, looked forward to Christ's mercy.

After God gave Moses the ten commandments, He instructed Moses on how to build a tent pavilion—a tabernacle. This was to contain the "ark of the covenant." You can see God's instructions to Moses on how to build the ark in Exodus 25:10–30. Moses was to place the tablets of stone with the ten commandments engraved on them in the ark. The lid of the ark was to be made of pure gold, with two guardian angels of pure gold. One angel was placed on each end of the ark, facing each other and looking down upon the place of mercy for our sins. The place of mercy for your sins is literally the "mercy seat" or the propitiation for your sins.

For those who accept Christ as Lord of their life, He gives grace as the substitute for our inability to keep the Law. The "ark of the covenant" points us toward Christ's death on the cross. The "covenant" was God's promise that He would provide a suitable substitute for sin. God's judgment under the Law was death.

Christ's death on the cross was a willful act of obedience to God the Father in order to fulfill the Law. He became the propitiation (atonement) for our sins. For those who do not accept Christ, the Law still applies, and they will be judged according to the Law and ultimately found guilty. If you think that this doesn't sound inclusive or fair, just remember that you are either living under "God's truth" or your own set of rules—believing "Satan's lie."

The blessings and promises of God are "truth" for those who are called according to His purposes. If anyone thinks he will spend eternity in heaven, he must live by God's truth. God, through Christ, created heaven and hell, our world, and the universe. Christ alone is worthy of judging each person and pronouncing judgment on those who have rejected Him. In John 10:9 (TLB), Christ said, "Yes, I am the Gate. Those who come in by way of the Gate will be saved and will go in and out and find green pastures." In verse 10 (TLB), He said, "The thief's purpose is to steal, kill and destroy. My purpose is to give life in all its fullness."

Chapter 8:
Believe in God the Creator—
Not the Creation

It is stated in the ten commandments, "Thou shall have no other gods before Me." God is a jealous God, and we must accept by faith that "He is" in order to be adopted into His family. The mountains, valleys, oceans, forests, and even the uniqueness of the barren wilderness can be appreciated for their beauty. But those things were not created to be worshiped. Neither should we worship planets, animals, or persons—living or dead.

Even in the most distant civilizations, you will find a belief in God. God placed within each of us a fundamental knowledge of Himself—a higher power—a belief in a spiritual presence. Without the knowledge of God's Word, we make something He created or material possessions our god.

If you were born with five major senses, you should thank God, who gave them to you. But there is another sense that needs to develop and mature; this is your conscience. It is our conscience that reveals to us that there is a God, or a higher power, that doesn't merely exist in the universe but exercises control over it. Your conscience is the gateway to your soul. It is a simple child-like faith that tells us to trust and have faith that our Father can take care of all of the difficulties that come our way. We begin to develop our conscience by seeking wisdom. We do that by seeking God's Word and reverence for the Lord.

> How does a man become wise? The first step
> is to trust and reverence the Lord! Only fools
> refuse to be taught. Listen to your father
> and mother. What you learn from them will
> stand you in good stead; it will gain you
> many honors.

Proverbs 1:7–9 (TLB)

=Your conscience can only be developed by seeking God's wisdom. Your conscience is God's searchlight that determines your intentions and motives. If your conscience is obedient to God and follows His outline for your life, it will lead to wisdom, common sense, knowledge, understanding, and fairness. All of these are more valuable than silver and gold because they lead to a fulfilled life through faith in Jesus Christ, our Redeemer. Romans 10:9 (TLB) states, "For if you tell others with your own mouth that Jesus Christ is your Lord and believe in your own heart that God has raised him from the dead, you will be saved." Romans 10:10 (TLB) says, "For it is by believing in his heart that a man becomes right with God; and with his mouth he tells others of his faith, confirming his salvation."

We each have a conscience, which defines and develops our spirit. You can begin to see a child's spirit develop at a very young age. A rebellious spirit will often be accompanied by a spirit of determination. Parents who are acutely aware of a child's rebellious spirit will want to first pray for God's guidance. Then they will want to drive out the rebellion while at the same time fostering the child's determination. "A youngster's heart is filled with rebellion, but punishment will drive it out of him" (Proverbs 22:15, TLB).

Rebellious children without boundaries will soon bring harm to themselves or to others. They have not matured enough to properly evaluate the consequences of their actions. It is the parent's responsibility to be persistent in defining established boundaries. A "don't do that" from across the room is not adequate correction for a child with a rebellious spirit. That is mere "projectile discipline," which simply is deflected by the armament of the strong-willed child. That armament is also resistant to repeated threats, increased volume, counting, and time-outs by the score.

You may find that time-outs allow for the child's artistic ability to be displayed on the walls and wallpaper.

Properly correcting such a child may hurt, but it will not harm the child. You may be saving their life. Foster their spirit of determination by providing challenging projects with age-appropriate difficulties and levels of success. If any of that sounds easy, you don't have a strong-willed rebellious child.

Chapter 9:
Jesus—Man and God

During His short three-year ministry on Earth, Jesus demonstrated His power and authority as He revealed His glory. He had authority over all things spiritual and physical because He was the creator. Jesus is God the Messiah. His ministry gave proof of His deity, and His death on the cross showed that He was man. He referred to Himself as "the Son of Man" and the "Son of God," capable of not only creating but also recreating. He did this by healing the lame, blind, and sick, and He even raised the dead. Jesus is the "light of the world," the "water," and the "bread of life."

The accounts of recorded miracles and signs and wonders were systematic and proof of His deity and His authority in heaven and on Earth.

Event	Scripture
Jesus is the light that shows men their sin, just as the law shined light on men's sin	John 3:18–19
Jesus' virgin birth was highlighted by kings bringing gifts with a star to guide them to Bethlehem.	Isaiah 7:14; Matthew 2:1–6; Luke 2:1–14

Event	Scripture
King Herod sent soldiers to Bethlehem and ordered them to kill every male child born in Bethlehem two years of age and younger.	Matthew 2:16
Jesus performed His first miracle by changing water into wine at a wedding in the village of Cana in Galilee.*	John 2:1–11
Jesus took a child's lunch consisting of loaves of bread and fish and fed thousands.	Matt.14:15–21; Matt.15:32–38; Luke 9:12–17; John 6:5–14
Jesus walked on water and calmed the wind.	Matt. 14:22–23; Mark 6:45–52; John 6:17–21
Jesus was a rabbi with full knowledge of the Scripture. The rabbi selected those he would teach. He selected the disciples and is selecting those who would believe and follow Him today.	John 13:18
Jesus healed the sick.	Matt. 9:20–22; Mark 5:25–34; Luke 8:43–48
Jesus knew what the people were thinking.	Matthew 9:4
Jesus caused the blind to see.	Matt. 20:29–34
Jesus cured the leper by touching him.	Mark 8:22–26; Mark 10:46–52; Luke 18:35–43; John 9:1–7

Event	Scripture
Jesus caused the lame to walk.	Matthew 8:1–4; Mark 1:40–45; Luke 5:12–15; Luke 17:11–19
Jesus told His disciples where to cast their nets to catch fish.	Luke 5:4–6
Jesus cast out demons.	Matt. 8:28–34; Matt. 12:22–23; Matt. 15:21–28
Jesus fulfilled the Scriptures.	Micah 5:2; Matthew 2:1–6; Matthew 2:17; Luke 2:1–20
Jesus healed the Roman captain's servant boy from miles away.	Matt. 8:5–13; Luke 7:1–10
Jesus healed the man from Capernaum's son while in Cana.	John 4:46–54
Jesus healed the mute man.	Matt. 9:32–33
Jesus told the lady at the well of her past.	John 4:17–18
Jesus raised Lazarus from the dead after he was in the grave for four days.	John 11:1–45
Jesus commanded the storm and sea to be still.	John 5:21
Jesus forgave sin.	Matt. 8:23–27
Jesus healed the paralytic.	Mark 4:35–41
Jesus hid as they were about to stone Him.	Luke 8:22–25

Event	Scripture
Jesus was absent from one place and appeared in another.	Matt. 9:1–2; Acts 10:43; John 5:22
Jesus knew the future.	Matthew 9:1–8; Luke 5:17–26
Jesus healed the soldier who came to arrest Him.	John 8:59
Jesus appeared in a locked room.	John 6:1–22
Jesus was obedient to the Father, and allowed Himself to be sacrificed to redeem man.	John 1:29–30 John 10:17–18
Jesus had power over death and raised Himself from the dead.	Matt. 28:1–10 John 10:18
Jesus will raise all who believe in Him at the last day.	Acts 2:22–32
Jesus ascended to heaven as watchful eyes observed.	Luke 24:50–51

*Jesus changed water into wine. Jesus' mother, Mary, said to Him, "They have no wine." Jesus replied, "Woman what have I to do with thee? Mine hour has not yet come." He was not chastising Mary for her statement; He simply was saying, "Woman, what am I going to do with you? You know My time has not yet come." I can almost see a smile on Mary's face, for she knew Jesus' compassion and said to the servants, "Do whatever He (Jesus) tells you to do." (See John 2:3–5). This is just as much a miracle by Mary because she knew that the child to whom she gave birth was also the Son of God. If Mary had not known that Jesus was the Son of God, she would have screamed at the cross that Jesus was a fraud in order to save His life.

Can we look at all that Jesus did while on Earth and

say that He was just a good man? Jesus' life and ministry are unparalleled in history. His authority over all things was demonstrated by His miracles and the fulfillment of prophecy. He is Lord over all, and yet He allowed His life's blood to be shed to wash away your sin. He redeemed all who are called according to His will and purpose. Is it any wonder our calendar is based upon the year of His birth?

His authority was not just for the three years of His earthly ministry but extends over all time. His authority and power are absolute over everything that occurs in our society today. He even uses the evil of this world to accomplish His will and purpose. Proverbs 16:4 (TLB), "The Lord has made everything for his own purposes—even the wicked for punishment."

No man can hasten the day of His return because the time is determined according to God's will and plan. Our life is equally secure when we are obedient to His will and purpose. The future is known to God as clearly as the past and present. He knew the temple would be destroyed, and He knows the future of His chosen people Israel. God knows the battles that will be fought, the lives that will be lost, and the outcome of wars. He knows the rivers and waters will turn to blood. He knows the sun, moon, and stars will fade away. He knows that Satan will be defeated and cast into the lake of fire. He knows all this because He sees the future with greater visual acuity than we see the present happenings in our world.

Christ was both man and God. He was born of water and blood and was crucified willingly on a cross for the forgiveness of sin. Yet He was God and showed His power over things of this earth, even death itself. He has left us His Holy Spirit, the Spirit of truth, to be our counselor and comforter.

When Christ gave us the holy Eucharist—partaking of the bread and wine symbolic of His body and blood, many of His followers could not accept this teaching and no longer followed Him. "From that time many of his disciples went back, and walked no more with him" (John 6:66, paraphrased by the author).

God has revealed that He will rapture those who are alive on Earth when He returns. He will also raise the dead in Christ. He knows that believers and unbelievers alike will bow their knees before Him and confess that Jesus Christ is Lord. His Word declares that He will set up a literal kingdom on a new earth and rule over all.

Chapter 10:
God's Wisdom for
Daily Living

God's Word is the very foundation of life and our ability to have wisdom, knowledge, and understanding, which will ultimately determine our ability to govern ourselves.

Our founding fathers had the foresight and strength of their convictions to frame a form of government. They formed a republic based on the Word of God. They were profoundly impacted by their personal commitment to establishing God's Word at the very center of their government's structure. I am sure it was not a coincidence that we have three branches of government—legislative, judicial, and executive.

The biblical basis for our structure and Judeo-Christian legal system has come under attack by those who would seek to alter the foundational principles in favor of their idea of a more modern, progressive government. There are those who seek to remove Christian symbols and references to God, such *as* "In God We Trust," on our currency. They want to do this, in spite of the fact that it is our national motto. Similar efforts have been made to remove prayer from sporting events—the pledge of allegiance, our national anthem, and the American flag.

Direct attacks on our First Amendment rights are brought to the courts in a cleverly fashioned way to present two positions that are both opposed to the First Amendment. A favorable decision on either position would set a new precedent and weaken the intent of our founders—thereby weakening the rights of "we the people."

Efforts to destroy our Constitution—the very foundation of a government of "we the people" have not been without success. Our Supreme Court Justices now look at case law as precedent in order to determine future decisions. This is done in spite of their oath to uphold the Constitution of the United States. It is as if each decision has papal blessing and authority and is thereby declared infallible. This will perpetuate one wrong decision onto the next set of circumstances and thereby continue the lineage of erroneous decisions.

Each time we fail to measure a decision by the founding principles of the Constitution, we weaken the Constitution to the point of destruction. How long will it take to replace our Constitution with the authority of the latest decision? You might argue that we have arrived at that point in the history of our country. The next appointee to the Supreme Court could change case law to effectively destroy the foundation of the Constitution.

"We the people are the rightful masters of both Congress and the Courts, not to overthrow the Constitution but to overthrow the men who pervert the Constitution" (Abraham Lincoln).

A carpenter needs a measuring device, such as a "standard" ruler, to measure and cut a board. The next cut and future cuts should be measured by the "standard" ruler. If he were to use the cut board as the standard for future cuts, it would not take long for future cuts to depart from the original "standard" ruler. We need to recognize and maintain the standards *of* "God's truth" and the Constitution as "absolute standards" which will not be deviated from for convenience or preference.

Our founding fathers would assuredly have looked at the abortion of an unborn child as murder by *their* "biblical standards" and Judeo-Christian laws. They would have reached this conclusion because God's Word was their "standard." They would have seen God's Word as an absolute, which cannot be changed by circumstances, convenience, or hardship, regardless of the consequences. To do otherwise would be to deny "God's truth" in favor of "Satan's lie."

Each decision that erodes our Constitution also serves to destroy God's Word as the foundation of our republic and moves us one step closer to rebellion, destruction, and chaos. We have been a blessed country because of our

Constitution and the fact that we have acknowledged our honor and dependence on a sovereign God.

Today, we view "fairness" as more important than justice because justice demands punishment for guilt. The scale of justice balances punishment and guilt. If our laws and courts decriminalize wrongful acts and remove the penalty, we think that we have removed guilt. But the only thing we have accomplished is to promote lawless behavior, chaos, and rebellion. "God's truth" is still an absolute that demands justice. Again we are weighing "God's truth" against "Satan's lie" of good and evil.

Choosing a lesser evil is still evil. We cannot justify wrong actions by calling it a greater good, social justice, or saying that "the end justifies the means." We may be able to prolong or discard punishment in the short term, but we are only promoting rebellion by tearing down necessary boundaries and consequences. We do this because of a prevalent philosophy of "fairness," thereby substituting "fairness" or the "greater good" for truth and justice.

When the government provides "rights" in the form of entitlements to the people, they do so at the risk of rebellion if the entitlements are ever withdrawn. The person or government that gives you rights and privileges can also be the one to withdraw the same as well as future rights. Today we have social security, welfare, unemployment, food stamps, housing assistance, health care, education, and many other programs for the benefit of contributors and citizens. Many view that these entitlements or rights should be extended to those who are non-citizens because it would be "unfair" not to share.

Its enemy's "fairness" soon replaces "God's truth" of justice and mercy. "Fairness" removes guilt because it justifies a person's actions by circumstances. Justice, however, requires personal responsibility and impartiality under the law, while "fairness" is arbitrary and emotionally based. "Fairness" will always be based on conditions, circumstances, and the opinion of the person making the decision. "Fairness" has no absolutes or standards as guidance and will promote chaos. "Fairness" will declare "God's truth" to be obsolete, antiquated, and lacking in its application to modern conditions and circumstances.

Justice requires that a person be held personally responsible for their actions by proper punishment and/or repentance and restitution. Mercy is God's privilege to extend to believers who would acknowledge His lordship. Justice finds us guilty when we violate "God's truth," and God alone can provide forgiveness and life through "mercy" to those of His calling.

We can forgive someone if they have offended us and, in so doing, show mercy to the offender. Parents can properly show forgiveness and mercy within their responsibility as parents. However, when government takes on the role of forgiveness and mercy, we see injustice, discrimination, and the ultimate destruction of the Law.

Chapter 11:
Proverbs—a Pathway
to Wisdom

Proverbs was written by King Solomon of Israel—David's son. God made King Solomon the wisest man to ever live because King Solomon asked for wisdom to govern His people, the children of Israel.

Let's take a look at Solomon's prayerful request.

> O Lord my God, now you have made me the
> king instead of my father David, but I am
> as a little child who doesn't know his way
> around. And here I am among your own
> chosen people, a nation so great that there
> are almost too many people to count! Give
> me an understanding mind so that I can gov-
> ern your people well and know the difference
> between what is right and what is wrong. For
> who by himself is able to carry such a heavy
> responsibility? The Lord was pleased with
> his reply and was glad that Solomon had
> asked for wisdom. So he replied, "Because
> you have asked for wisdom in governing my
> people and you haven't asked for a long life,

or riches for yourself, or the defeat of your
enemies—yes, I'll give you what you asked
for! I will give you a wiser mind than anyone
else has ever had or ever will have! And I will
also give you what you didn't ask for—riches
and honor! And no one in all the world will
be as rich and famous as you for the rest of
your life! And I will give you a long life if you
follow me and obey my laws as your father
David did."

1 Kings 3:7–14 (TLB)

God did as He promised, and King Solomon reigned
for forty years. His wealth was unprecedented in history
as he amassed upwards of 500 tons of gold and had 700
wives and 300 concubines. He built the temple that God
would not allow David to build, which housed the ark of
the covenant. He may be better known for his writings of
Proverbs, written to teach his people how to live and to
teach even the simple-minded how to become wise.

Wisdom comes from God, and it is His prerogative to
give it to those who would ask for and seek wisdom as they
would seek a precious gift.

Every young man who listens to me and
obeys my instructions will be given wis-

dom and good sense. Yes, if you want better insight and discernment, and are searching for them as you would for lost money or hidden treasure, then wisdom will be given you and knowledge of God himself; you will soon learn the importance of reverence for the Lord and of trusting him. For the Lord grants wisdom! His every word is a treasure of knowledge and understanding. He grants good sense to the godly—his saints. He is their shield, protecting them and guarding their pathway. He shows how to distinguish right from wrong, how to find the right decision every time. For wisdom and truth will enter the very center of your being.

Proverbs 2:1–10 (TLB)

The words of Solomon were recorded in the book of Proverbs in couplets, which he intended to use to teach his people how to live and how to become wise. These nuggets of truth, as he referred to them, were specially written to help young people to become wise in order to avoid the pitfalls of evil. The guidance provided by the Proverbs will give happiness and long life. It will teach you how to avoid the path of destruction caused by greed, disobedience, and evil.

Proverbs should be taught to every child as they begin to develop their decision-making processes. It should be taught at home, in churches, and in our schools as the framework for building positive character qualities. Proverbs give the contrasting benefits of proper godly decisions and the consequences of poor choices. Good and evil (adverse consequences) are contrasted in each proverb.

Proverbs can make even the simple-minded wise by developing their conscience to allow "God's truth" to fill their minds and soul. When "God's truth" and wisdom are our chosen pathways, we can begin to develop character qualities that prepare us for life and protect us from evil and unnecessary danger. Beginning with our conscience as a guide, we add wisdom through "God's truth" and add positive character qualities which protect and prosper us as we gain knowledge and understanding.

Chapter four of Proverbs tells us just how important a parent's guidance is, particularly a father's instruction to his son.

This excerpt is from the New International Version (NIV) translation of the Bible which retains the poetry of chapters 1–9.

> Listen, my son, to a father's instruction
> [discipline]: pay attention and gain under-
> standing [experiential knowledge]. I give
> you sound learning [education], so do not

forsake my teaching. When I was a boy in my father's house, still tender, and an only child of my mother, he taught me and said, "Lay hold of my words with all your heart [intellect]; keep my commands, and you will live. Get wisdom, get understanding [good judgment and common sense]; do not forget my words or swerve from them. Do not forsake wisdom, and she will protect you; love her, and she will watch [rescue and guard] over you. Wisdom is supreme; therefore get wisdom. Though it cost all you have, get understanding. Esteem her, and she will exalt you; embrace her, and she will honor you. She will set a garland of grace on your head and present you with a crown of splendor." Listen, my son, accept what I say, and the years of your life will be many. I will guide you in the way of wisdom and lead you along straight paths. When you walk, your steps will not be hampered; when you run, you will not stumble. Hold on to instruction, do not let it go; guard it well, for it is your life. Do not set foot on the path of the wicked or walk in the way of evil men. Avoid it, do not travel on it; turn from it and go on your way. For they cannot sleep till they do evil; They are robbed of slumber till they make someone fall. They eat the bread of wickedness and drink the wine of violence. The path of the righteous is like the first gleam of dawn, shining ever brighter till the full light of day. But the way of the wicked is like deep darkness; they do not know what makes them stumble. My son, pay attention to what I say; listen closely to my words. Do not let them out of your sight, keep them within your heart; For they are life to those who find them and health to a man's whole body. Above all else, guard your heart, for it is the well-spring of life. Put away perversity from your mouth; keep corrupt talk far from your lips. Let your eyes look straight ahead, fix your gaze directly before you. Make level paths for your feet and take only ways that are firm. Do not swerve to the right or to the left; keep your foot from evil.

Proverbs 4 (NIV)

God's Pathway

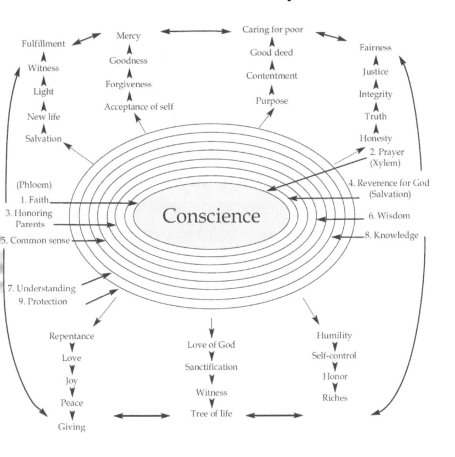

Proverbs 11:30 (KJV), "The fruit of the righteous is a tree of life; and he that winneth souls is wise."

Comparing the growth rings of a tree to the pathway of righteousness for a believer in God's Word.

In chart "A"—God's Pathway, we see that character is built within a person, similar to the growth rings in a cross-section of a tree. The water and nutrients from the soil are transferred from the roots through the xylem to the leafy extremities of a tree. The leaves produce life-giving energy through photosynthesis and send this energy back to the root system through the phloem. In a similar fashion, our prayers flow from our faith root system (xylem) to God. God's response to our prayers is life-giving strength that flows back to us (phloem) and increases our faith as it provides growth in character, wisdom, and understanding. The growth rings of a tree symbolize character growth in a believer.

Conscience is the knowledge of God that He has placed in each of us. Romans 1:18–20 (TLB) states,

> But God shows his anger from heaven
> against all sinful, evil men who push away
> the truth from them. For the truth about
> God is known to them instinctively; God has
> put his knowledge in their hearts. Since ear-
> liest times men have seen the earth and sky
> and all God made, and have known of his
> existence and great eternal power. So they
> will have no excuse when they stand before
> God at Judgment Day.

Your conscience is God's searchlight into your heart and soul, where He sees your intent and motivation. Your conscience can only protect you by seeking God's wisdom. If your conscience is obedient to "God's Word" and follows His outline and pathway for your life, He will lead you by His Holy Spirit to wisdom, common sense, knowledge, and discernment. Following wisdom will provide a long life filled with honor and satisfaction because you have fulfilled a purpose pleasing not only to yourself but also to God. All of this is more valuable than gold or silver because the Holy Spirit provides righteousness and the assurance of God's promise of eternal life by faith in Jesus Christ, our Redeemer.

God gave you a conscience as a warning system to caution your mind and heart to avoid things that are evil and potentially harmful. If you ignore the cautionary prodding of your conscience by allowing sinful thoughts to be dwelt on in your mind, you are allowing a "toehold" to be established. You may soon find yourself in a habit or "foothold" of seeking greater satisfaction and fulfillment of your thoughts and desires. Next, you develop an addiction to needing more and more for self-gratification to satisfy your mind, body, or emotions. A thought has matured into a "stronghold" over your life and now controls you rather than you being in control of it. You have allowed your conscience to be seared, and it no longer protects you by its warning system. The door is now open to allow all manner of evil and demonic behavior to enter your soul and body.

Faith is complete reliance and trust in "God's truth" even though you have not seen it with your eyes or experienced it in a physical sense. Romans 1:17 (TLB) says,

> This Good News tells us that God makes us ready for heaven—makes us right in God's sight—when we put our faith and trust in Christ to save us. This is accomplished from start to finish by faith. As the Scripture says it, "The man who finds life will find it through trusting God."

Even the faith we have is not of ourselves but comes from God's Holy Spirit. Therefore it is not something that should cause us to be boastful. The eleventh chapter of Hebrews is a summary of how Old Testament believers exercised their faith in God. "What is faith? It is the confident assurance that something we want is going to happen. It is the certainty that what we hope for is waiting for us, even though we cannot see it up ahead" (Hebrews 11:1, TLB).

We can visualize a pet scratching at a door, attempting to get to the other side—not knowing what is on the other side but desiring to be with his master.

> But all these things that I once thought very
> worthwhile—now I've thrown them all away
> so that I can put my trust and hope in Christ
> alone. Yes, everything else is worthless when
> compared with the priceless gain of knowing
> Christ Jesus my Lord. I have put aside all
> else, counting it worth less than nothing, in
> order that I can have Christ, and become one
> with him, no longer counting on being saved
> by being good enough or by obeying God's
> laws, but by trusting Christ to save me; for
> God's way of making us right with himself
> depends on faith—counting on Christ alone.
>
> **Philippians 3:7–9 (TLB)**

Prayer—in the Old Testament, God was not accessible to the common man. God only spoke to His prophets and patriarchs, but man approached God through the high priest. When Solomon built the temple, which was a replica of the temple in heaven, God dwelt in the Holy of Holies. This was a veiled section that was entered only once a year by the high priest to present a blood sacrifice for the sins of man. But when Christ was crucified, the veiled curtain was split from top to bottom; therefore, no longer do we access God through the high priest but through Christ, whose blood was the only acceptable sacrifice for the sins of man.

Christ is our advocate to the Father because He is alive and seated at the right hand of the Father God. We can offer our prayers to a Holy God because Christ is our mediator. No longer is it necessary for the high priest to intercede for us. Christ is our worthy intercessor to the Father, not only to hear our prayers but also to respond to our spirit according to His will for our lives as a loving Father.

> And in the same way—by our faith—the
> Holy Spirit helps us with our daily problems
> and in our praying. For we don't even know
> what we should pray for nor how to pray as
> we should, but the Holy Spirit prays for us
> with such feeling that it cannot be expressed
> in words.
>
> **Romans 8:26 (TLB)**

Honoring parents will protect you from the imminent dangers of life and the influence of evil men who can steal your youth and set you on a pathway that leads to destruction. Listen to the warnings of your parents as a shield of protection. (See Proverbs four in this chapter.)

Common sense, knowledge, and understanding will be added as levels of protection to the degree that you study and learn "God's truth." The core values that you establish for your life will open your life to God's blessings, which He will shower upon you. "And since, when we were his enemies, we were brought back to God by the death of his Son, what blessings he must have for us now that we are his friends and he is living in us!" (Romans 5:10, TLB).

The outer circle of chart "A" represents God's assurance that He will richly reward and give success to your efforts by adding the fruit of your labor to your positive character qualities.

Character is added upon character as layers of strength and protection as we make proper choices. This is a building process that begins with the fear of the Lord and respect for parental guidance. Chart "A" is not a fixed chart, and you might want to develop your own chart as you apply the proverbs to your life. Each of us has differing strengths and weaknesses, which God can use to cause us to focus on different promises and blessings. Respect and honoring God's Word will result in good works and benefits for this life and for eternity.

If you were to draw a circle around chart "A," you would find that "Satan's lie" tries to deceive us at every point by temptations and by empty promises which he cannot fulfill. Chart "B" demonstrates the consequences of following Satan's lies—His empty promises and temptations to disobey God's truth.

Labyrinth of Evil

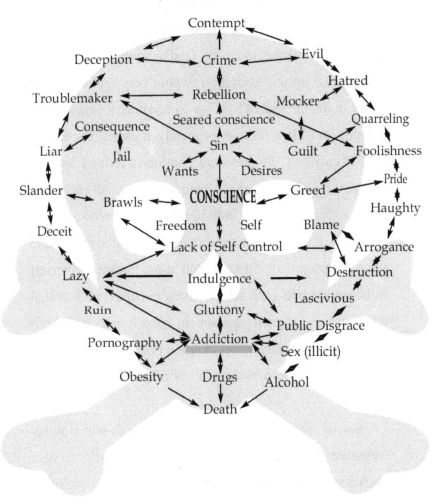

Do you find yourself in this chart?

Are you heading down a pathway that leads to death and destruction? This is a graphic description of the pathways of evil encouraged by "Satan's lie." Satan's objective for your life is to steal, kill, and destroy, and he will provide every empty promise to entice you to follow his "lie."

Solomon gives particular attention to sexual sin and temptation. Disobedience to God's warning to abstain from sexual sin will even destroy your very soul and could result in death. "Satan's lie" is to consider a sexual relationship outside marriage as merely a casual encounter. This is currently the prevalent opinion in today's society. Television and Hollywood glamorize the casual encounter as an expression of an individual's sexual prowess. But in reality, it can destroy your marriage, your witness, and your integrity. Only a fool would allow himself or herself to be drawn into such self-destructive behavior. A sexual affair outside of marriage can rip apart homes and families and permanently affect children and their hope for the future. Yet men and women fall blindly into the snares of the trap.

Sexual sin leaves a scar that never heals and is never forgotten. Sin, especially sexual sin, leaves a scar on your conscience that Satan can bring to your mind in an effort to destroy your witness and reputation, even when there has been repentance and forgiveness.

It is easy to lure young people with the thought of material goods and money. The availability of drugs and alcohol is an enticement to fit in with the crowd. They diminish the thought process and inhibitions to the extent that stealing, dealing drugs, prostitution, and acts of violence are regarded as just a means to an end. Parents, particularly Christian parents, have a grave responsibility to protect, educate, and bring up a child in the ways of the Lord. This is not an easy task in today's society, with the influence of wrongful thinking so prevalent.

A child can be enticed into the wrong crowd, where he will experience sudden consequences that are well beyond his ability to handle and may be devastating to his life. In today's society, there are gangs that entice children to become a part of their lawless behavior. The innocence of a child is soon lost if drugs and violence against citizens or competing gangs cause severe injury or death. An otherwise innocent child can find themselves thrust into an adult court being tried as an adult or possibly the victim of violence. A young person's attitude of invincibility only adds to their potential peril.

Satan may not be omniscient (all-knowing) as God is; however, he is quite capable of observing our interests and actions in order to prey on our weaknesses. Just as "Google" can observe what we are viewing and determine our interests and then suggest sights of interest, Satan can find our weak areas and exploit them with lascivious thoughts and desires. Charles Stanley explains that Satan endeavors to get a "toehold" of sin in your life in order to gain a "foothold." Continuous pursuit will lead to a "stronghold" of harmful behavior that may eventually lead to your destruction.

If you depend on an Ouija board, Tarot cards, or horoscopes for daily guidance instead of "God's Word," you will soon find yourself on a pathway that will lead to mysticism and the occult. It would be wisdom on your part to divert your eyes and attention away from things that will direct your conscience to thoughts of evil. Get-rich schemes and gambling are Satan's empty promises to provide something that God does not consider profitable for your well-being.

Because God wants to shower His grace and wisdom upon those whom He has called to be His children, He will reveal His desires for your life. He can do so by putting a thought in your heart or revealing wisdom and understanding from His Word that will not only protect you but will prosper you beyond your capabilities and human effort. He will cause circumstances in your life to be in your favor and of personal benefit. Psalm 37:23 (TLB) says, "The steps of good men are directed by the Lord. He delights in each step they take." We refer to these types of happenings as "divine providence." This is being at the right place at the right time or being detained for just a few moments, thus preventing or avoiding a possible disaster. God's grace is His unmerited favor upon your daily life as well as your soul. When God reveals a purpose for your life, He is giving you a divine "gift." We are able to look back on a loss or failure and, in retrospect, see that *God turned it for our good.* "And we know that all that happens to us is working for our good if we love God and are fitting into his plan" (Romans 8:28, TLB).

Knowing that God is leading us by His wisdom, grace, and Holy Spirit gives us hope in situations that may look hopeless. You can be strengthened by the knowledge that He loves you enough to guide your steps and keep you from falling even when the path is rough and rocky. He does this not because of any goodness we may possess but because of His love for us. He desires to protect us as a father would protect his children.

Chapter 12:
A Good Man

We look at a man's behavior and speech to determine his character and to ascertain what kind of person he is. God knows the heart of man and sees his desires even before they are carried out. A good man is one who desires to obey God in his heart. Wisdom is given to such a man as his common sense directs his thoughts, actions, and reverence to obey God's Word. Therefore, when an opportunity presents itself for unearned gain, lascivious thoughts, or a desire to do wrong, he recognizes it as a temptation to sin, to be disobedient to God's will for his life. A good man's common sense will cause him to flee from danger. Wisdom will protect him as it delivers him from doing wrong. The evil man, the one who has planned to do wrong in his heart, sees an opportunity and acts on the temptation to his demise.

Heaven is not an entitlement that all receive when our life on Earth is over. Hell is if we reject God's grace.

> The Lord will not let a good man starve to death, nor will he let the wicked man's riches continue forever. …The good man is covered with blessings from head to foot, but an evil man inwardly curses his luck. We

all have happy memories of good men gone to their reward, but the names of the wicked men stink after them. ...A good man has firm footing, but a crook will slip and fall. ...There is living truth in what a good man says, but the mouth of the evil man is filled with curses. ... The good man's earnings advance the cause of righteousness. The evil man squanders his on sin. ...When a good man speaks, he is worth listening to, but the words of fools are a dime a dozen. A godly man gives good advice, but the rebel is destroyed by lack of common sense. ... The wicked man's fears will all come true and so will the good man's hopes. Disaster strikes like a cyclone and the wicked are whirled away. But the good man has a strong anchor. ... Reverence for God adds hours to each day; so how can the wicked expect a long, good life? The hope of good men is eternal happiness; the hopes of evil men are all in vain. God protects the upright but destroys the wicked. The good shall never lose God's blessing, but the wicked shall lose everything. The good man gives wise advice, but the liar's counsel is shunned. The upright speak what is helpful; the wicked speak rebellion.

**Proverbs 10:3, 6–7, 9, 11, 16,
20–21, 24–25, 27–32 (TLB)**

A good man is guided by his honesty; the evil man is destroyed by his dishonesty. … Good people are directed by their honesty; the wicked shall fall beneath their load of sin. The good man's goodness delivers him; the evil man's treachery is his undoing. … God rescues good men from danger while letting the wicked fall into it. Evil words destroy; godly skill rebuilds. The whole city celebrates a good man's success—and also the godless man's death. The good influence of godly citizens causes a city to prosper, but the moral decay of the wicked drives it downhill. To quarrel with a neighbor is foolish; a man with good sense holds his tongue. …Without wise leadership, a nation is in trouble; but with good counselors there is safety. …Honor goes to kind and gracious women, mere money to cruel men. Your own soul is nourished when you are kind; it is destroyed when you are cruel. The evil man gets rich for the moment, but the good man's reward lasts forever. The good man finds life; the evil man, death. The Lord hates the stubborn but delights in those who are good. You can be very sure the evil man will not go unpunished forever. And you can also

be very sure God will rescue the children of
the godly. ...The good man can look forward
to happiness, while the wicked can expect
only wrath. It is possible to give away and
become richer! It is also possible to hold
on too tightly and lose everything. Yes, the
liberal man shall be rich! By watering others,
he waters himself. ...Trust in your money
and down you go! Trust in God and flourish
as a tree! ...If the righteous receive their due
on earth, how much more the ungodly and
the sinner!

**Proverbs 11:3, 5–6, 8–12, 14,
16–21, 23–25, 28 (TLB)**

Proverbs 3:31 (NIV)

To learn, you must want to be taught. To refuse reproof is stupid. The Lord blesses good
men and condemns the wicked. Wickedness
never brings real success; only the godly have
that. ...A good man's mind is filled with honest thoughts; an evil man's mind is crammed
with lies. The wicked accuse; the godly defend. The wicked shall perish; the godly shall
stand. ...A good man is concerned for the
welfare of his animals, but even the kindness

of godless men is cruel. …Crooks are jealous
of each other's loot, while good men long to
help each other. …A fool thinks he needs no
advice, but the wise man listens to others.
…A good man is known by his truthfulness;
a false man by deceit and lies. …Deceit fills
hearts that are plotting for evil; joy fills the
hearts that are planning for good. No real
harm befalls the good, but there is constant
trouble for the wicked. …The good man
asks advice from friends; the wicked plunge
ahead—and fall. …The path of the godly
leads to life. So why fear death?

**Proverbs 12:1–3, 5–7, 10,
12, 15, 17, 20–21, 26, 28 (TLB)**

The good man wins his case by careful
argument; the evil-minded only wants to
fight. …A good man hates lies; wicked men
lie constantly and come to shame. A man's
goodness helps him all through life, while
evil men are being destroyed by their wickedness. …The good man's life is full of light.
The sinner's road is dark and gloomy. …
Despise God's Word and find yourself in
trouble. Obey it and succeed. …Curses chase

sinners, while blessings chase the righteous!
When a good man dies, he leaves an inheritance to his grandchildren; but when a
sinner dies, his wealth is stored up for the
godly. ...The good man eats to live, while the
evil man lives to eat.

Proverbs 13:2, 5–6, 9, 13, 21–22, 25 (TLB)

The common bond of rebels is their guilt.
The common bond of godly people is goodwill. ...The work of the wicked will perish;
the work of the godly will flourish. ...The
backslider gets bored with himself; the godly
man's life is exciting. ...Evil men shall bow
before the godly. ...Those who plot evil shall
wander away and be lost, but those who plan
good shall be granted mercy and quietness.
...The godly have a refuge when they die, but
the wicked are crushed by their sins.

Proverbs 14:9, 11, 14, 19, 22, 32 (TLB)

The Lord is watching everywhere and keeps
his eye on both the evil and the good. ...
There is treasure in being good, but trouble
dogs the wicked. Only the good can give
good advice. Rebels can't. The Lord hates the

gifts of the wicked but delights in the prayers of his people. ...A lazy fellow has trouble all through life; the good man's path is easy! ... The road of the godly leads upward, leaving hell behind. ...A good man thinks before he speaks; the evil man pours out his evil words without a thought. The Lord is far from the wicked, but he hears the prayers of the righteous.

Proverbs 15:3, 6–8, 19, 24, 28–29 (TLB)

We can make our plans, but the final outcome is in God's hands. ...Commit your work to the Lord, then it will succeed. ... When a man is trying to please God, God makes even his worst enemies to be at peace with him. ...The path of the godly leads away from evil; he who follows that path is safe. ... God blesses those who obey him; happy the man who puts his trust in the Lord. ...White hair is a crown of glory and is seen most among the godly.

Proverbs 16:1, 3, 7, 17, 20, 31 (TLB)

Proverbs 17:6 (TLB), "An old man's grandchildren are his crowning glory. A child's glory is his father."

Pride ends in destruction; humility ends in honor. ...The intelligent man is always open to new ideas. In fact, he looks for them. ...There are "friends" who pretend to be friends, but there is a friend who sticks closer than a brother.

Proverbs 18:12, 15, 24 (TLB)

Many beg favors from a man who is generous; everyone is his friend! ...Kindness makes a man attractive. And it is better to be poor than dishonest. Reverence for God gives life, happiness, and protection from harm.

Proverbs 19:6, 22–23 (TLB)

It is an honor for a man to stay out of a fight. Only fools insist on quarreling. ...Deep in a man's spirit [conscience] is the knowledge of his need for God, and a man of understanding will draw it out. ...Since the Lord is directing our steps, why try to understand everything that happens along the way? ... The glory of young men is their strength; of old men, their experience.

Proverbs 20:3, 24, 29 (TLB)
Proverbs 20:5 (paraphrased by the author)

God is more pleased when we are just and fair than when we give him gifts. A man is known by his actions. An evil man lives an evil life; a good man lives a godly life. A good man loves justice, but it is a calamity to evil-doers. The man who tries to be good, loving and kind finds life, righteousness and honor. The lazy man longs for many things but his hands refuse to work. He is greedy to get, while the godly love to give! An evil man is stubborn, but a godly man will reconsider.

Proverbs 21:3, 8, 15, 21, 25–26, 29

If you must choose, take a good name rather than great riches; for to be held in loving esteem is better than silver and gold. A prudent man foresees the difficulties ahead and prepares for them; the simpleton goes blindly on and suffers the consequences. Keep away from angry, short-tempered men, lest you learn to be like them and endanger your soul.

Proverbs 22:1, 3, 24–25

Proverbs 23:23–25 (TLB), "Get the facts at any price, and hold on tightly to all the good sense you can get. The father of a godly man has cause for joy—what pleasure a wise son is! So give your parents joy!"

> O evil man, leave the upright man alone and quit trying to cheat him out of his rights. Don't you know that this good man, though you trip him up seven times, will each time rise again? But one calamity is enough to lay you low. …My son, watch your step before the Lord and the king, and don't associate with radicals. For you will go down with them to sudden disaster, and who knows where it will end?
>
> **Proverbs 24:15–16, 21–22 (TLB)**

> If a godly man compromises with the wicked, it is like polluting a fountain or muddying a spring. Just as it is harmful to eat too much honey, so also it is bad for men to think about all the honors they deserve!
>
> **Proverbs 25:26–27 (TLB)**

Proverbs 27:21 (TLB), "The purity of silver and gold can be tested in a crucible, but man is tested by his reaction to men's praise."

The wicked flee when no one is chasing
them! But the godly are bold as lions! ...
When the godly are successful, everyone is
glad. When the wicked succeed, everyone
is sad. ...Good men will be rescued from
harm, but cheaters will be destroyed.

Proverbs 28:1, 12, 18 (TLB)

With good men in authority, the people
rejoice; but with the wicked in power, they
groan. ...The good man knows the poor
man's rights; the godless don't care. ...The
godly pray for those who long to kill them.
...When rulers are wicked, their people are
too; but good men will live to see the tyrant's
downfall. ...The good hate the badness of the
wicked. The wicked hate the goodness of the
good.

Proverbs 29:2, 7, 10, 16, 27 (TLB)

Chapter 13:
Anger/Temper/Rage

Under the laws of Moses the rule was, 'If
you murder, you must die.' But I [Jesus] have
added to that rule and tell you that if you are
only angry [some translations say without
cause], even in your own home, you are in
danger of judgment! If you call your friend
an idiot, you are in danger of being brought
before the court. And if you curse him, you
are in danger of the fires of hell.

Matthew 5:21–22 (TLB)

Being angry or having a quick temper has an immediate effect on your life and possibly your life span. You see
it on the highways as road rage, in bars as stabbings and
shootings. An angry person looks for something or someone to vent his anger, to kick, hit, or destroy, in order to
demonstrate just how angry he is.

Anger is demonstrated by a selfish person who wants
his or her way and simply does not care about anyone else.
A display of anger often causes another to back down or
give up their desires. The person showing anger will use
this to manipulate and get his way, even when it serves to

damage another's self-esteem.

Beware of a person with anger issues. A quick temper can escalate rapidly to a rage. An angry person also lacks self-control and will attack the thing that he knows is most important to another person. For this reason, identify an angry person and do not engage them in controversial issues. They will vent against family and friends first. Drugs and alcohol lower a person's inhibitions and can propel an angry person to rage, even regarding minor issues.

If you have anger issues, seek help. Pray for God's help in surrendering your will to His will. Allow God's Holy Spirit to calm your anger by the application of memorized scripture (Proverbs 21:23). Avoid friendship with an angry person; you could be a victim of his rage.

Proverbs 15:18 (TLB), "A quick-tempered man starts fights; a cool-tempered man tries to stop them."

Proverbs 16:32 (TLB), "It is better to be slow-tempered than famous; it is better to have self-control than to control an army."

Proverbs 17:14 (TLB), "It is hard to stop a quarrel once it starts, so don't let it begin."

Proverbs 18:19 (TLB), "It is harder to win back the friendship of an offended brother than to capture a fortified city. His anger shuts you out like iron bars."

The king's anger is as dangerous as a lion's.

But His approval is as refreshing as the dew
on grass. ...A short-tempered man must
bear his own penalty; you can't do much to
help him. If you try once, you must try a
dozen times!

Proverbs 19:12, 19 (TLB)

Proverbs 20:3, 22 (TLB), "It is an honor for a man to
stay out of a fight. Only fools insist on quarreling. ...Don't
repay evil for evil. Wait for the Lord to handle the matter."

Proverbs 21:14, 23 (TLB), "An angry man is silenced
by giving him a gift! ...Keep your mouth closed and you'll
stay out of trouble."

Proverbs 22:24–25 (TLB), "Keep away from angry,
short-tempered men, lest you learn to be like them and endanger your soul."

Don't demand an audience with the king as
though you were some powerful prince. It is
better to wait for an invitation rather than to
be sent back to the end of the line, publicly
disgraced! Don't be hotheaded and rush to
court. You may start something you can't
finish and go down before your neighbor in
shameful defeat. So discuss the matter with
him privately. Don't tell anyone else, lest he

accuse you of slander and you can't withdraw
what you said. …Be patient and you will
finally win, for a soft tongue can break hard
bones. As surely as a wind from the north
brings cold, just as surely a retort [sharp
answer] causes anger!

Proverbs 25:6–10, 15, 23 (TLB)

Proverbs 26:21 (TLB), "A quarrelsome man starts
fights as easily as a match sets fire to paper."

A rebel shouts in anger; a wise man holds his
temper in and cools it. …There is more hope
for a fool than for a man of quick temper.
…A hot-tempered man starts fights and gets
into all kinds of trouble.

Proverbs 29:11, 20, 22 (TLB)

Chapter 14:
Blessings—the Beatitudes

Blessed are the poor in spirit, for theirs is the
kingdom of heaven. Blessed are those who
mourn, for they will be comforted. Blessed
are the meek, for they will inherit the earth.
Blessed are those who hunger and thirst for
righteousness, for they will be filled. Blessed are the merciful, for they will be shown
mercy. Blessed are the poor in heart, for they
will see God. Blessed are the peacemakers,
for they will be called children of God. Blessed are those who are persecuted because of
righteousness, for theirs is the kingdom of
heaven. Blessed are you when people insult
you, persecute you and falsely say all kinds
of evil against you because of me. Rejoice
and be glad, because great is your reward in
heaven, for in the same way they persecuted
the prophets who were before you.

Matthew 5:3–12 (NIV)

Are you seeking God's blessings? Which of these do

you desire? Do you want to be poor in spirit, to mourn, to be meek, to hunger and thirst for righteousness, to be merciful, a peacemaker, or to be persecuted? Or do you want to be insulted or verbally attacked by people saying evil against you? Heaven is surely the antithesis of this world. Christ said we should rejoice if people say evil things against us because we are living a Christian life. Surely your reward is great if you suffer because of Him.

This is not what comes to mind when we pray for God's blessings on our friends or us. We tend to pray for material things, health, or things of monetary value. We want a good job with pay that will provide comfort, a nice home, and a car, along with vacations and travel. Isn't that the "American dream?"

Do you pray for God's will or for your will? When you are concerned with doing God's will and are obedient to His Word, He will give you the desires of your heart or change the desires of your heart, just as He did for Solomon.

It is more important to focus on the things that are eternal than to pursue the things of this world. A dying man has no interest in material possessions, even if he has spent a lifetime accumulating them. The only valuable he can take with him is his relationship with God through Christ.

How do you stress the importance of the godly pathway of life to a developing child? Solomon prayed for wisdom to govern the children of Israel and God blessed him because of his request. Our prayer ought to be, "God, grant me Your wisdom that I may do Your will." For if your purpose in life is to do His will, He will shower blessings upon you, and you will find fulfillment. When God shows you His will and purpose for your life, you have received a wonderful gift.

Proverbs 3:13–14 (NIV), "Blessed is the man who finds wisdom, the man who finds understanding, for she is more profitable than silver and yields better returns than gold."

Gold and silver are this world's standard of wealth but of no value in heaven. With wisdom and understanding, you will discover what is considered valuable for eternity.

Ecclesiastes 11:8 (TLB) says, "If a person lives to be very old, let him rejoice in every day of life, but let him also remember that eternity is far longer and that everything down here is futile in comparison."

God's blessings are on the upright.

> The good man is covered with blessings from head to foot, but an evil man inwardly curses his luck. …The Lord's blessing is our greatest wealth. All our work adds nothing to it! …
> The wicked man's fears will all come true

and so will the good man's hopes. ...Reverence for God adds hours to each day; so how can the wicked expect a long, good life? The hope of good men is eternal happiness; the hopes of evil men are all in vain. God protects the upright but destroys the wicked. The good shall never lose God's blessings, but the wicked shall lose everything.

Proverbs 10:6, 22, 24, 27–30 (TLB)

God rescues good men from danger while letting the wicked fall into it. ...The whole city celebrates a good man's success—and also the godless man's death. The good influence of godly citizens causes a city to prosper, but the moral decay of the wicked drives it downhill. ...Honor goes to kind and gracious women, mere money to cruel men. Your own soul is nourished when you are kind; it is destroyed when you are cruel. The evil man gets rich for the moment, but the good man's reward lasts forever. ...You can be very sure the evil man will not go unpunished forever. And you can also be very sure God will rescue the children of the godly. ... People curse the man who holds his grain for higher prices, but they bless the man who

sells it to them in their time of need. If you
search for good, you will find God's favor; if
you search for evil, you will find his curse.

**Proverbs 11:8, 10–11,
16–18, 21, 26–27 (TLB)**

The Lord blesses good men and condemns
the wicked. …A worthy wife is her husband's
joy and crown; the other kind corrodes his
strength and tears down everything he does.
…No real harm befalls the good, but there is
constant trouble for the wicked. …The path
of the godly leads to life. So why fear death?

Proverbs 12:2, 4, 21, 28 (TLB)

A man's goodness helps him all through life,
while evil men are being destroyed by their
wickedness. …The good man's life is full of
light. The sinner's road is dark and gloomy.
…Curses chase sinners, while blessings chase
the righteous!

Proverbs 13:6, 9, 21 (TLB)

The work of the wicked will perish; the work
of the godly will flourish. …The backslider
gets bored with himself; the godly man's life
is exciting. …He that despiseth his neighbor

sinneth: but he that hath mercy on the poor, happy is he. Those who plot evil shall wander away and be lost, but those who plan good shall be granted mercy and quietness. …Reverence for God gives a man deep strength; his children have a place of refuge and security. Reverence for the Lord is a fountain of life; its waters keep a man from death. …A relaxed attitude lengthens a man's life; jealousy rots it away. …The godly have a refuge when they die, but the wicked are crushed by their sins. …Godliness exalts a nation, but sin is a reproach to any people.

Proverbs 14:11, 14, 22, 26–27, 30, 32, 34 (TLB),

Proverbs 14:21 (KJV)

There is treasure in being good, but trouble dogs the wicked. …The road of the godly leads upward, leaving hell behind. The Lord destroys the possessions of the proud but cares for widows. …Dishonest money brings grief to all the family, but hating bribes brings happiness. …The Lord is far from the wicked, but he hears the prayers of the righteous. If you profit from constructive crit-

icism, you will be elected to the wise men's
hall of fame.

Proverbs 15:6, 24–25, 27, 29, 31 (TLB)

Commit your work to the Lord, then it will
succeed. …When a man is trying to please
God, God makes even his worst enemies to
be at peace with him. …We should make
plans—counting on God to direct us. …The
path of the godly leads away from evil; he
who follows that path is safe. …God blesses
those who obey him; happy the man who
puts his trust in the Lord. …Wisdom is a
fountain of life to those possessing it, but a
fool's burden is his folly.

Proverbs 16:3, 7, 9, 17, 20, 22 (TLB)

The Lord is a strong fortress. The godly run
to him and are safe. …Pride ends in destruction; humility ends in honor. …The man
who finds a wife finds a good thing; she is a
blessing to him from the Lord.

Proverbs 18:10, 12, 22

He who loves wisdom loves his own best
interest and will be a success. …A father can
give his sons homes and riches, but only the

Lord can give them understanding wives. ...
Keep the commandments and keep your life;
despising them means death. ...There are
many devices in a man's heart; nevertheless
the counsel of the Lord [God's Word and the
leading of the Holy Spirit], that shall stand.
...Reverence for God gives life, happiness,
and protection from harm.

**Proverbs 19:8, 14, 16, 23 (TLB),
Proverbs 19:21 (KJV)**

It is a wonderful heritage to have an honest
father. ...If you have good eyesight and good
hearing, thank God who gave them to you.
...Since the Lord is directing our steps, why
try to understand everything that happens
along the way? ...The glory of young men is
their strength; of old men their experience.

Proverbs 20:7, 12, 24, 29 (TLB)

Proverbs 21:31 (TLB), "Go ahead and prepare for the
conflict, but victory comes from God."

True humility and respect for the Lord lead a
man to riches, honor, and long life. ...Teach
a child to choose the right path, and when
he is older, he will remain upon it. ...Hap-

py is the generous man, the one who feeds
the poor. …Do you know a hard-working
man? He shall be successful and stand before
kings!

Proverbs 22:4, 6, 9, 29 (TLB)

Proverbs 23:17–18 (TLB), "Don't envy evil men but continue to reverence the Lord all the time, for surely you have a wonderful future ahead of you. There is hope for you yet!"

Rescue those who are unjustly sentenced
to death; don't stand back and let them
die. Don't try to disclaim responsibility by
saying you didn't know about it. For God,
who knows all hearts, knows yours, and he
knows you knew! And he will reward everyone according to his deeds. …When you
enjoy becoming wise, there is hope for you!
A bright future lies ahead! …but blessings
shall be showered on those who rebuke sin
fearlessly.

Proverbs 24:11–12, 14, 25 (TLB)

Proverbs 25:21–22 (TLB), "If your enemy is hungry, give him food! If he is thirsty, give him something to drink! This will make him feel ashamed of himself, and God will reward you."

Proverbs 26:2 (TLB), "An undeserved curse has no effect. Its intended victim will be no more harmed by it than by a sparrow or swallow flitting through the sky."

When there is moral rot within a nation, its government topples easily; but with honest, sensible leaders there is stability. ...A curse on those who lead astray the godly. But men who encourage the upright to do good shall be given a worthwhile reward. ...A man who refuses to admit his mistakes can never be successful. But if he confesses and forsakes them, he gets another chance. Blessed is the man who reveres God, but the man who doesn't care is headed for serious trouble. ... Good men will be rescued from harm, but cheaters will be destroyed. ...The man who wants to do right will get a rich reward. But the man who wants to get rich quick will quickly fail. ...Greed causes fighting; trusting God leads to prosperity. A man is a fool to trust himself! But those who use God's wisdom are safe. If you give to the poor, your needs will be supplied! But a curse upon those who close their eyes to poverty.

**Proverbs 28:2, 10, 13–14, 18,
20, 25–27 (TLB)**

When rulers are wicked, their people are too; but good men will live to see the tyrant's downfall. Discipline your son and he will give you happiness and peace of mind. Where there is ignorance of God, crime runs wild; but what a wonderful thing it is for a nation to know and keep his laws. …Fear of man is a dangerous trap, but to trust in God means safety.

Proverbs 29:16–18, 25 (TLB)

Chapter 15:
Common Sense

If you follow the directions from "God's Word," you will receive wisdom and common sense.

Common sense isn't very common. We have moved away from the "truth" to such a degree that we look at two untruths and try to determine which of the two is true. If we desire to know the truth, we need to consult the source of truth, God's Word.

David said in Psalm 40:8 (NIV), "I desire to do your will, O my God; your law is within my heart." When we seek God's wisdom, He pours out common sense and knowledge of Himself. By trusting in Him and in His Word, our common sense serves to protect us from harm and gives us discernment.

We live in a world of instant gratification and the ability to have what we cannot afford "if we act now." When our vision is myopic, we abandon our common sense and give way to our desires.

To become indebted beyond our ability to pay makes us slaves to the lender. We try to justify it, but we are borrowing from future earnings to purchase today's desire. It is only later, when we tire of our purchase, that we question our judgment and common sense.

Applying our common sense, guided by God's Word and His Holy Spirit, will lead to knowledge, wisdom, and understanding. Refusing to use or listen to common sense will lead a person to foolishness and potentially harmful conduct.

> Every young man who listens to me and obeys my instructions will be given wisdom and good sense. Yes, if you want better insight and discernment, and are searching for them as you would for lost money or hidden treasure, then wisdom will be given you, and knowledge of God himself; you will soon learn the importance of reverence for the Lord and of trusting him. For the Lord grants wisdom! His every word is a treasure of knowledge and understanding. He grants good sense to the godly—his saints. He is their shield, protecting them and guarding their pathway. He shows how to distinguish right from wrong, how to find the right decision every time. For wisdom and truth will enter the very center of your being [conscience], filling your life with joy. You will be given the sense to stay away from evil men who want you to be their partners

in crime—men who turn from God's ways
to walk down dark and evil paths and exult
in doing wrong, for they thoroughly enjoy
their sins. Everything they do is crooked and
wrong.

Proverbs 2:1–15 (TLB)

If you follow God's directions, you will have common sense and wisdom.

Men with common sense are admired as
counselors; those without it are beaten as
servants. ...The good man's earnings advance the cause of righteousness. The evil
man squanders his on sin. Anyone willing
to be corrected is on the pathway to life.
Anyone refusing has lost his chance. ...Don't
talk so much. You keep putting your foot
in your mouth. Be sensible and turn off the
flow! When a good man speaks, he is worth
listening to, but the words of fools are a dime
a dozen. A godly man gives good advice,
but a rebel is destroyed by lack of common
sense. ...Reverence for God adds hours to
each day; so how can the wicked expect a
long, good life?

Proverbs 10:13, 16–17, 19–21, 27 (TLB)

The Lord hates cheating and delights in honesty. …A good man is guided by his honesty; the evil man is destroyed by his dishonesty. …Without wise leadership, a nation is in trouble; but with good counselors there is safety. Be sure you know a person well before you vouch for his credit! Better refuse than suffer later.

Proverbs 11:1, 3, 14–15 (TLB)

Proverbs 12:8 (TLB), "Everyone admires a man with good sense, but a man with a warped mind is despised."

A man's goodness helps him all through life, while evil men are being destroyed by their wickedness. …The good man's life is full of light. The sinner's road is dark and gloomy. …The advice of a wise man refreshes like water from a mountain spring. Those accepting it become aware of the pitfalls on ahead. A man with good sense is appreciated. A treacherous man must walk a rocky road. … An unreliable messenger can cause a lot of trouble. Reliable communication permits progress.

Proverbs 13:6, 9, 14–15, 17 (TLB)

A mocker never finds the wisdom he claims

he is looking for, yet it comes easily to the
man with common sense. ...The wise man
looks ahead. The fool attempts to fool himself and won't face facts. ...The simpleton is
crowned with folly; the wise man is crowned
with knowledge. ...Wisdom is enshrined in
the hearts of men of common sense, but it
must shout loudly before fools will hear it.

Proverbs 14:6, 8, 18, 33 (TLB)

A quick-tempered man starts fights; a
cool-tempered man tries to stop them. ...
If a man enjoys folly, something is wrong!
The sensible stay on the pathway of right.
...Everyone enjoys giving good advice, and
how wonderful it is to be able to say the right
things at the right time! The road of the godly leads upward, leaving hell behind. ...Dis-
honest money brings grief to all the family,
but hating bribes brings happiness.

Proverbs 15:18, 21, 23–24, 27 (TLB)

Iniquity is atoned for by mercy and truth;
evil is avoided by reverence for God. ...We
should make plans—counting on God to
direct us. ...The wise man is known by his
common sense, and a pleasant teacher is the

best.

Proverbs 16:6, 9, 21 (TLB)

A rebuke to a man of common sense is more
effective than a hundred lashes on the back
of a rebel. ...It is poor judgment to countersign another's note, to become responsible
for his debts. ...Wisdom is the main pursuit
of sensible men, but a fool's goals are at the
ends of the earth!

Proverbs 17:10, 18, 24 (TLB)

Proverbs 18:15, 17 (TLB), "The intelligent man is always open to new ideas. In fact, he looks for them. ...Any
story sounds true until someone tells the other side and sets
the record straight."

Proverbs 19:16, 27 (TLB), "Keep the commandments
and keep your life; despising them means death. ...Stop
listening to teaching that contradicts what you know is
right."

Proverbs 19:27 (NIV), "Stop listening to instruction,
my son, and you will stray from the words of knowledge."

Good sense is far more valuable than gold or
precious jewels. It is risky to make loans to
strangers! ...It is foolish and rash to make a

promise to the Lord before counting the cost.
...A man's conscience [spirit] is the Lord's
searchlight exposing his hidden motives.

Proverbs 20:15–16, 25, 27 (TLB)

God is more pleased when we are just and
fair than when we give him gifts. ...The wise
man learns by listening; the simpleton can
only learn by seeing scorners punished. ...
The man who strays away from common
sense will end up dead! ...The wise man
saves for the future, but the foolish man
spends whatever he gets.

Proverbs 21:3, 11, 16, 20 (TLB)

A prudent man foresees the difficulties
ahead and prepares for them; the simpleton
goes blindly on and suffers the consequences. True humility and respect for the Lord
lead a man to riches, honor, and long life.
The rebel walks a thorny, treacherous road;
the man who values his soul will stay away.
...The Lord preserves the upright but ruins
the plans of the wicked. ...Listen to this wise
advice, follow it closely, for it will do you
good, and you can pass it on to others: Trust
in the Lord. ...Unless you have extra cash

on hand, don't countersign a note. Why risk everything you own? They'll even take your bed!

Proverbs 22:3–5, 12, 17–19, 26–27 (TLB)

Don't weary yourself trying to get rich. Why waste your time? For riches can disappear as though they had the wings of a bird. …Don't waste your breath on a rebel. He will despise the wisest advice. …Don't refuse to accept criticism; get all the help you can. …My son, how I will rejoice if you become a man of common sense. Yes, my heart will thrill to your thoughtful, wise words. Don't envy evil men but continue to reverence the Lord all the time, for surely you have a wonderful future ahead of you. There is hope for you yet! O my son, be wise and stay in God's paths. …Listen to your father's advice and don't despise an old mother's experience. Get the facts at any price, and hold on tightly to all the good sense you can get.

Proverbs 23:4–5, 9, 12, 15–19, 22–23 (TLB)

Don't envy godless men; don't even enjoy their company. …A wise man is mightier than a strong man. Wisdom is mightier than

112

strength. ...Develop your business first before building your house.

Proverbs 24:1, 5, 27 (TLB)

Don't be hotheaded and rush to court! You
may start something you can't finish and go
down before your neighbor in shameful defeat. So discuss the matter with him privately. ...It is a badge of honor to accept valid
criticism. ...Don't visit your neighbor too
often, or you will outwear your welcome!

Proverbs 25:8–9, 12, 17 (TLB)

Proverbs 27:2, 11 (TLB), "Don't praise yourself; let
others do it! ...My son, how happy I will be if you turn out
to be sensible! It will be a public honor to me."

To complain about the law is to praise wickedness. To obey the law is to fight evil. ...A
man who refuses to admit his mistakes can
never be successful. But if he confesses and
forsakes them, he gets another chance. ...In
the end, people appreciate frankness more
than flattery. ...Greed causes fighting; trusting God leads to prosperity.

Proverbs 28:4, 13, 23, 25 (TLB)

Chapter 16:
Without Common Sense
(Fool)

Proverbs 1:7 (KJV), "The fear of the Lord is the beginning of knowledge: but fools despise wisdom and instruction."

They say you should never try to teach a pig how to sing because it is a total waste of your time and only serves to frustrate the pig. Such is the case when you attempt to instruct a fool who is caught up in his folly. A person who is so focused on his personal wants that he refuses counsel will ignore every cautionary sign. He likely will look at his pleasure or self-indulgence as his only worthy pursuit. Try to change his thinking or behavior, and you will be told, "The only one I am hurting is myself, so what business is it of yours?" Isn't this freedom, after all?

> The fool says in his heart, "There is no God."
> They are corrupt, their deeds are vile; there is
> no one who does good. The Lord looks down
> from heaven on all mankind to see if there
> are any who understand, any who seek God.
>
> **Psalm 14:1–2 (NIV)**

It is pleasant to listen to wise words, but a
fool's speech brings him to ruin. Since he
begins with a foolish premise, his conclusion
is sheer madness. A fool knows all about the
future and tells everyone in detail! But who
can really know what is going to happen? A
fool is so upset by a little work that he has no
strength for the simplest matter.

Ecclesiastes 10:12–15 (TLB)

A fool is one who lives out his life just as "Satan's lie" outlines, doing what appears right in his own eyes. He exercises his will by choosing between good and evil according to what gives him the greatest satisfaction. A fool is often easy to recognize because he treats any effort on your part to redirect him with rebuke and name-calling. He will also return to you for help when consequences come upon him because he knows you possess wisdom and understanding. Then he will readily accept your help but refuse to change his patterns of behavior and thinking. He continues to assert his personal freedom and free will that gave him permission to believe "Satan's lie."

The wise man is glad to be instructed, but
a self-sufficient fool falls flat on his face. ...
Men with common sense are admired as
counselors; those without it are beaten as

servants. A wise man holds his tongue. Only a fool blurts out everything he knows; that only leads to sorrow and trouble. ...To hide hatred is to be a liar; to slander is to be a fool. ...A godly man gives good advice, but a rebel is destroyed by lack of common sense. ...A fool's fun is being bad; a wise man's fun is being wise! God protects the upright but destroys the wicked. ...The upright speak what is helpful; the wicked speak rebellion.

Proverbs 10:8, 13–14, 18,
21, 23, 29, 32 (TLB)

To quarrel with a neighbor is foolish; a man with good sense holds his tongue. A gossip goes around spreading rumors, while a trustworthy man tries to quiet them. ...The fool who provokes his family to anger and resentment will finally have nothing worthwhile left. He shall be the servant of a wiser man.

Proverbs 11:12–13, 29 (TLB)

A fool thinks he needs no advice, but a wise man listens to others. A fool is quick-tempered; a wise man stays cool when insulted. ...A wise man doesn't display his knowledge, but a fool displays his foolishness.

Proverbs 12:15–16, 23 (TLB)

Self-control means controlling the tongue! A
quick retort can ruin everything. …A wise
man thinks ahead; a fool doesn't and even
brags about it! …It is pleasant to see plans
develop. That is why fools refuse to give
them up even when they are wrong.

Proverbs 13:3, 16, 19 (TLB)

A wise woman builds her house, while a
foolish woman tears hers down by her own
efforts. …If you are looking for advice, stay
away from fools. The wise man looks ahead.
The fool attempts to fool himself and won't
face facts. …Before every man there lies a
wide and pleasant road that seems right but
ends in death. …Only a simpleton believes
everything he's told! A prudent man un-
derstands the need for proof. A wise man is
cautious and avoids danger; a fool plunges
ahead with great confidence. A short-tempered man is a fool. He hates the man who is
patient. The simpleton is crowned with folly;
the wise man is crowned with knowledge.
…Wise men are praised for their wisdom;
fools are despised for their folly. …Wisdom

is enshrined in the hearts of men of common sense, but it must shout loudly before fools will hear it.

Proverbs 14:1, 7–8, 12, 15–18, 24, 33 (TLB)

Only a fool despises his father's advice; a wise son considers each suggestion. ...If a man enjoys folly, something is wrong! The sensible stay on the pathways of right. ...A good man thinks before he speaks; the evil man pours out his evil words without a thought.

Proverbs 15:5, 21, 28 (TLB)

It is safer to meet a bear robbed of her cubs than a fool caught in his folly. ...Sinners love to fight; boasting is looking for trouble. ...Wisdom is the main pursuit of sensible men, but a fool's goals are at the ends of the earth! [Chaos.] ...The man of few words and settled mind is wise, therefore, even a fool is thought to be wise when he is silent. It pays him to keep his mouth shut.

Proverbs 17:12, 19, 24, 27–28 (TLB)

Proverbs 18:6–7, 13 (TLB), "A fool gets into constant fights. His mouth is his undoing! His words endanger him. …What a shame—yes, how stupid!—to decide before knowing the facts!"

Proverbs 19:3, 10 (TLB), "A man may ruin his chances by his own foolishness and then blame it on the Lord! … It doesn't seem right for a fool to succeed or for a slave [servant] to rule over princes!"

> Wine gives false courage; hard liquor leads
> to brawls; what fools men are to let it master
> them, making them reel drunkenly down the
> street! …It is an honor for a man to stay out
> of a fight. Only fools insist on quarreling. …
> God puts out the light of the man who curses
> his father or mother. …It is foolish and rash
> to make a promise to the Lord before count-
> ing the cost.
>
> **Proverbs 20:1, 3, 20, 25 (TLB)**

Proverbs 21:20, 24 (TLB), "The wise man saves for the future, but the foolish man spends whatever he gets. … Mockers are proud, haughty and arrogant."

Proverbs 22:14 (TLB), "A prostitute is a dangerous trap, those cursed of God are caught in it."

Proverbs 24:10 (TLB), "You are a poor specimen if you can't stand the pressure of adversity."

Proverbs 25:28 (TLB), "A man without self-control is as defenseless as a city with [no security] broken-down walls."

> Honor doesn't go with fools any more than snow with summertime or rain with harvesttime! …When arguing with a rebel, don't use foolish arguments as he does, or you will become as foolish as he is! Prick his conceit with silly replies! …In the mouth of a fool a proverb becomes as useless as a paralyzed leg. …As a dog returns to his vomit, so a fool repeats his folly. There is one thing worse than a fool, and that is a man who is conceited. …Yanking a dog's ears is no more foolish than interfering in an argument that isn't any of your business.
>
> **Proverbs 26:1, 4–5, 7, 11–12, 17 (TLB)**

> A sensible man watches for problems ahead and prepares to meet them. The simpleton never looks and suffers the consequences. The world's poorest credit risk is the man who agrees to pay a stranger's debts. If you shout a pleasant greeting to a friend too early in the morning, he will count it as a curse! … You can't separate a rebel from his foolish-

ness though you crush him to powder.

Proverbs 27:12–14, 22 (TLB)

A man who refuses to admit his mistakes
can never be successful. But if he confesses
and forsakes them, he gets another chance.
Blessed is the man who reveres God, but the
man who doesn't care is headed for serious
trouble. …Only a stupid prince will oppress
his people, but a king [leader] will have a
long reign if he hates dishonesty and bribes.
…Giving preferred treatment to rich people
is a clear case of selling one's soul for a piece
of bread. Trying to get rich is evil and leads
to poverty. …A man who robs his parents
and says, "What's wrong with that?" is no
better than a murderer.

Proverbs 28:13–14, 16, 21–22, 24 (TLB)

The man who is often reproved but refuses
to accept criticism will suddenly be broken
and never have another chance. …A wise
son makes his father happy, but a lad who
hangs around with prostitutes disgraces him.
…There is no use arguing with a fool. He
only rages and scoffs, and tempers flare. …
There is more hope for a fool than for a man

of quick temper. ...A man who assists a thief must really hate himself! For he knows the consequences but does it anyway.

Proverbs 29:1, 3, 9, 20, 24 (TLB)

Chapter 17:
Counsel

If you honestly desire to know God's will and direction for your life, it is well to seek the counsel of others. However, do not neglect to seek wisdom and understanding from God's Word and the prompting of His Holy Spirit as it speaks to your conscience.

Proverbs 12:15, "A fool thinks he needs no advice, but a wise man listens to others."

> Plans go wrong with too few counselors;
> many counselors bring success. Everyone
> enjoys giving good advice, and how wonderful it is to be able to say the right thing at the
> right time! ...The Lord hates the thoughts
> of the wicked but delights in kind words.
> ...A good man thinks before he speaks; the
> evil man pours out his evil words without a
> thought. ...If you profit from constructive
> criticism, you will be elected to the wise
> men's hall of fame. But to reject criticism is
> to harm yourself and your own best interest.
> Humility and reverence for the Lord will
> make you both wise and honored.
>
> **Proverbs 15:22–23, 26, 28, 31–33 (TLB)**

God will help the king [leader] to judge the people fairly; there need be no mistakes. ...The wise man is known by his common sense, and a pleasant teacher is the best. ... Kind words are like honey—enjoyable and helpful.

Proverbs 16:10, 21, 24 (TLB)

A true friend is always loyal, and a brother is born to help in time of need. ...The man of few words and settled mind is wise; therefore, even a fool is thought to be wise when he is silent. It pays him to keep his mouth shut.

Proverbs 17:17, 27–28 (TLB)

A wise man's words express deep streams of thought. It is wrong for a judge to favor the wicked and condemn the innocent. ...What a shame—yes, how stupid!—to decide before knowing the facts! ...Any story sounds true until someone tells their side and sets the record straight. ...Ability to give wise advice satisfies like a good meal!

Proverbs 18:4–5, 13, 17, 20 (TLB)

It is dangerous and sinful to rush into the unknown. …Get all the advice you can and be wise the rest of your life. There are many devices in a man's heart; nevertheless the counsel [authority of God's Word and Holy Spirit] of the Lord, that shall stand.

Proverbs 19:2, 20 (TLB),
Proverbs 19:21 (KJV)

Proverbs 20:5 (KJV), "Counsel [knowledge of God] in the heart of man is like deep water; but a man of understanding will draw it out."

Proverbs 20:18 (TLB), "Don't go ahead with your plans without the advice of others; don't go to war until they agree."

Proverbs 21:5, 18 (TLB), "Steady plodding brings prosperity; hasty speculation brings poverty. …The wicked will finally lose; the righteous will finally win."

Listen to this wise advice; follow it closely,
for it will do you good, and you can pass
it along to others: Trust in the Lord. In the
past, haven't I been right? Then believe what
I am telling you now and share it with others.

Proverbs 22:17–21 (TLB)

Proverbs 23:9, 12 (TLB), "Don't waste your breath on a rebel. He will despise the wisest advice. …Don't refuse to accept criticism; get all the help [knowledge] you can."

> Don't go to war without wise guidance; there
> is safety in many counselors. Wisdom is too
> much for a rebel. He'll not be chosen as a
> counselor. ...You are a poor specimen if you
> can't stand the pressure of adversity. ...It is
> an honor to receive a frank reply.
>
> **Proverbs 24:6–7, 10, 26 (TLB)**

> Don't demand an audience with the king as
> though you were some powerful prince. It is
> better to wait for an invitation rather than to
> be sent back to the end of the line, publicly
> disgraced! ...It is a badge of honor to accept
> valid criticism.
>
> **Proverbs 25:6–7, 12 (TLB)**

Proverbs 27:17 (TLB), "A friendly discussion is as stimulating as the sparks that fly when iron strikes iron."

Proverbs 29:26 (TLB), "Do you want justice? Don't fawn on the judge, but ask the Lord for it!"

Chapter 18:
Curse of God

The curse of God is on the wicked, but his
blessing is on the upright. The Lord mocks at
mockers, but helps the humble. The wise are
promoted to honor, but fools are promoted
to shame.

Proverbs 3:33–35 (TLB)

It seems unlikely that we would purposely choose
God's curse to be on our life because His hand can be very
strong against us. However, when we disobey His commandments, we choose His curse.

I am giving you the choice today between
God's blessings or God's curse! There will be
blessing if you obey the commandments of
the Lord your God which I am giving you
today, and a curse if you refuse them and
worship the gods of these other nations.

Deuteronomy 11:26–28 (TLB)

If you repay evil for good, a curse is upon your home.
If you pursue other gods and seek the spirit world through
a medium, psychics, or horoscope, you are inviting a curse

upon your life and home. If you possess stolen property or possessions from ill-gotten gain—you are in danger of a curse from God because He hears the prayers of those who have suffered a loss. God calls us to resist the devil, not invite him into our minds and spirit. Satan's demons are real, and they will possess you and control you if you invite them in. Disobedience to God's laws is a curse upon your life and well-being and all that you seek to accomplish.

> Reverence for God adds hours to each day;
> so how can the wicked expect a long, good
> life? The hope of good men is eternal hap-
> piness; the hopes of evil men are all in vain.
> God protects the upright but destroys the
> wicked.
>
> **Proverbs 10:27–29 (TLB)**

> God rescues good men from danger while
> letting the wicked fall into it [danger]. ...
> Your own soul is nourished when you are
> kind; it is destroyed when you are cruel. ...
> The good man finds life; the evil man, [finds]
> death. The Lord hates the stubborn but de-
> lights in those who are good. You can be very
> sure the evil man will not go unpunished
> forever. And you can be very sure God will
> rescue the children of the godly. ...People

curse the man who holds his grain for higher prices, but they bless the man who sells it to them in their time of need. If you search for good, you will find God's favor; if you search for evil, you will find his curse.

Proverbs 11:8, 17, 19–21, 26–27 (TLB)

The Lord blesses good men and condemns the wicked. …The worthy wife is her husband's joy and crown; the other kind [unworthy wife] corrodes his strength and tears down everything he does.

Proverbs 12:2, 4 (TLB)

A man's goodness helps him all through life, while evil men are being destroyed by their wickedness. …A man with good sense is appreciated. A treacherous man must walk a rocky road. …If you refuse criticism, you will end in poverty and disgrace; if you accept criticism, you are on the road to fame. …Curses chase sinners, while blessings chase the righteous!

Proverbs 13:6, 15, 18, 21 (TLB)

A wise woman builds her house, while a foolish woman tears hers [house] down by her own efforts. ...The backslider gets bored with himself; the godly man's life is exciting. ...Those who plot evil shall wander away and be lost, but those who plan good shall be granted mercy and quietness. ...A relaxed attitude lengthens a man's life, jealousy rots it [a man's life] away. ...The godly have a refuge when they die, but the wicked are crushed by their sins. ...Godliness exalts a nation, but sin is a reproach to any people.

Proverbs 14:1, 14, 22, 30, 32, 34

Gentle words cause life and health; griping brings discouragement. ...The Lord hates the gifts of the wicked but delights in the prayers of his people. The Lord despises the deeds of the wicked but loves those who try to be good. If they stop trying, the Lord will punish them; if they rebel against that punishment, they will die. ...The Lord destroys the possessions of the proud but cares for widows. The Lord hates the thoughts of the wicked but delights in kind words. ...The Lord is far from the wicked, but he hears the prayers of the righteous. ...If you profit from

constructive criticism, you will be elected
to the wise men's hall of fame. But to reject
criticism is to harm yourself and your own
best interests.

**Proverbs 15:4, 8–10, 25–26,
29, 31–32 (TLB)**

The Lord has made everything for his own
purposes—even the wicked for punishment.
Pride disgusts the Lord. Take my word for
it—proud men shall be punished. ...Before
every man there lies a wide and pleasant
road he thinks is right, but it ends in death.
...Idle hands are the devil's workshop; idle
lips are his mouthpiece.

Proverbs 16:4–5, 25, 27 (TLB)

Mocking the poor is mocking the God who
made them. He [God] will punish those who
rejoice at others' misfortunes. ...The wicked
live for rebellion; they [the wicked] shall be
severely punished. ...If you repay evil for
good, a curse is upon your home. ...The Lord
despises those who say that bad is good and
good is bad. ...An evil man is suspicious of
everyone and tumbles into constant trouble.

Proverbs 17:5, 11, 13, 15, 20 (TLB)

Proverbs 18:3 (TLB), "Sin brings disgrace [loss of reputation, integrity, and shame]."

Proverbs 18: 7 (KJV), "A fool's mouth is his destruction, and his lips are the snare of his soul."

Proverbs 18:12 (TLB), "Pride ends in destruction; humility ends in honor."

Proverbs 19:16, 26 (TLB), "Keep the commandments and keep your life; despising them [the commandments] means death. ...A son who mistreats his father or mother is a public disgrace."

> The Lord despises every kind of cheating.
> ...If you love sleep, you will end in poverty.
> Stay awake, work hard, and there will be
> plenty to eat! ...Some men enjoy cheating,
> but the cake they buy with such ill-gotten
> gain will turn to gravel in their mouths. ...
> God puts out the light of the man who curses
> his father or mother. ...The Lord loathes all
> cheating and dishonesty.
>
> **Proverbs 20:10, 13, 17, 20, 23 (TLB)**

> Steady plodding brings prosperity; hasty
> speculation brings poverty. ...Because the
> wicked are unfair, their violence boomerangs
> and destroys them. ...God, the Righteous
> One, knows what is going on in the homes

of the wicked and will bring the wicked to judgment. He who shuts his ears to the cries of the poor will be ignored in his own time of need. ...A good man loves justice, but it is a calamity to evildoers. ...The wicked will finally lose; the righteous will finally win. ... God loathes the gifts of evil men, especially if they are trying to bribe him! No one believes a liar, but everyone respects the words of an honest man.

Proverbs 21:5, 7, 12–13, 15, 18, 27–28 (TLB)

A prudent man foresees the difficulties ahead and prepares for them; the simpleton goes blindly on and suffers the consequences [of not seeing difficulties ahead]. ...Just as the rich rule the poor, so the borrower is servant to the lender. The unjust tyrant will reap disaster, and his reign of terror shall end. ... The Lord preserves the upright but ruins the plans of the wicked. ...A prostitute [unfaithful woman] is a dangerous trap; those cursed of God are caught in it. ...He who gains by oppressing the poor or by bribing the rich shall end in poverty. ...Don't rob the poor and sick! For the Lord is their defender. If you injure them, he will punish you. Keep

away from angry, short-tempered men, lest
you learn to be like them and endanger your
soul.

Proverbs 22:3, 7–8, 12, 14, 16, 22–25 (TLB)

Don't steal the land of defenseless orphans
by moving their ancient boundary marks,
for their Redeemer is strong; he himself will
accuse you. …O my son, trust my advice—
stay away from prostitutes. For a prostitute
is a deep and narrow grave. Like a robber,
she waits for her victims as one after another
become unfaithful to their wives. …Don't let
the sparkle and the smooth taste of strong
wine deceive you. For in the end it bites like
a poisonous serpent; it stings like an adder.
You will see hallucinations and have delirium tremens, and you will say foolish, silly
things that would embarrass you no end
when sober.

Proverbs 23:10–11, 26–28, 31–33 (TLB)

Don't envy the wicked. Don't covet his
riches. For the evil man has no future; his
light will be snuffed out. My son, watch
your step before the Lord and the king, and
don't associate with radicals. For you will

go down with them to sudden disaster, and who knows where it all will end? ...He who says to the wicked, "You are innocent," shall be cursed by many people of many nations." ...Then, as I looked, I learned this lesson: "A little extra sleep, A little more slumber, A little folding of the hands to rest" means that poverty will break in upon you suddenly like a robber and violently like a bandit.

Proverbs 24:19–22, 24, 32–33 (TLB)

Proverbs 25:28 (TLB), "A man without self-control is as defenseless as a city with broken-down walls [country without secure borders]."

Proverbs 26:27 (TLB), "The man who sets a trap for others will get caught in it himself. Roll a boulder down on someone, and it will roll back and crush you."

A sensible man watches for problems ahead and prepares to meet them. The simpleton never looks [for problems] and suffers the consequences. ...If you shout a pleasant greeting to a friend too early in the morning, he will count it as a curse! ...Ambition and death are alike in this: neither is ever satisfied.

Proverbs 27:12, 14, 20 (TLB)

When there is moral rot within a nation, its government topples easily; but with honest, sensible leaders there is stability. ...A curse on those who lead astray the godly. But men who encourage the upright to do good shall be given a worthwhile reward. ...A man who refuses to admit his mistakes can never be successful. But if he confesses and forsakes them, he gets another chance. Blessed is the man who reveres God, but the man who doesn't care [about God] is headed for serious trouble. ...A murderer's conscience will drive him to hell. Don't stop him! Good men will be rescued from harm, but cheaters will be destroyed. ... The man who wants to do right will get a rich reward. But the man who wants to get rich quick will quickly fail. Giving preferred treatment to rich people is a clear case of selling one's soul for a piece of bread. Trying to get rich quick is evil and leads to poverty. ...Greed causes fighting; trusting God leads to prosperity. ...If you give to the poor, your needs will be supplied! But a curse upon those who close their eyes to poverty.

Proverbs 28:2, 10, 13–14, 17–18, 20–22, 25, 27 (TLB)

The man who is often reproved but refuses to accept criticism will suddenly be broken and never have another chance. ...A wicked ruler will have wicked aides on his staff. …When rulers are wicked, their people are too; but good men will live to see the tyrant's downfall. …Where there is ignorance of God, crime runs wild; but what a wonderful thing it is for a nation to know and keep his laws. …Fear of man is a dangerous trap, but to trust in God means safety.

Proverbs 29:1, 12, 16, 18, 25 (TLB)

Proverbs 30:10–12 (TLB), "Never falsely accuse a man to his employer, lest he curse you for your sin. There are those who curse their father and mother and feel themselves faultless despite their many sins."

Chapter 19:
Discipline and Punishment

There is likely no better example of ignoring God's truth than in the area of how we are taught to discipline our children.

Doctors Spock and Freud have deflected our focus away from biblical teachings and focused on a child's self-esteem and attachment to parents as being of greater priority. What we are able to learn from child psychology is of great benefit in parenting, but we must not allow it to replace the truth of God's Word.

Our world today has an emphasis on protecting or building a child's self-esteem. This is placed at the pinnacle of priorities in disciplining—or refusing to discipline our children. So much so that it is often difficult to determine who is the parent and who is the child. When you see children demanding and directing their parents, you know that the world has turned upside down and God's truth is being ignored. Following the pathway of a godless child, psychology has produced undisciplined adults from undisciplined children. Because parents have failed to teach responsibility, we now have adults advocating that we *take* from the people who have worked for what they have and give to those less fortunate—which serves to perpetuate the lack of responsibility. The philosophy of the world is to remove the consequences of disobedience and bad behavior.

Let's look at what God's Word tells us in Hebrews.

> After all, you have never yet struggled
> against sin and temptation until you sweat
> great drops of blood. [As Christ did.] And
> have you quite forgotten the encouraging
> words God spoke to you, his child? He said,
> "My son, don't be angry when the Lord pun-
> ishes you. Don't be discouraged when he has
> to show you where you are wrong. For when
> he punishes you, it proves that he loves you.
> When he whips you, it proves you are really
> his child."
>
> **Hebrews 12:4–6 (TLB)**

God's correction can be gentle or severe depending on our response and need for protection and safety. A shepherd would sometimes find it necessary to break the leg of a lamb that would consistently stray away from the flock. The shepherd would then carry the lamb on his shoulders. When the lamb's leg healed, he would stay with the shepherd because he had developed such an attachment and love. Parents, don't neglect to discipline your children. It proves you love them and want to ensure their protection and development. Proper discipline may hurt them, but it will keep them from harm.

Have you noticed that when God disciplines you that the intensity increases as you consistently refuse to heed His correction? Each subsequent behavioral adjustment impacts you to a greater degree than the last. This only serves to assure you that He loves you because He is quick to discipline one of His own.

Discipline is used in three different ways.

1. Discipline can be patterns of behavior that are self-imposed for personal development, hygiene, knowledge, health, weight control, etc.

2. The second usage is closely related to the first. Businesses have discipline rules or standards of operation. Government and military have tactical or strategic disciplines.

3. Discipline can be a form of punishment or correction often imposed by parents, society, government, and God in the form of a consequence or penalty.

    All three disciplines can be found in Proverbs.

Proverbs 13:24 (TLB), "If you refuse to discipline your son, it proves you don't love him; for if you love him, you will be prompt to punish them."

The Lord despises the deeds of the wicked
but loves those who try to be good. If they
stop trying, the Lord will punish them; if
they rebel against that punishment, they will
die. A sensible son gladdens his father. A
rebellious son saddens his mother.

Proverbs 15:9–10, 20 (TLB)

Proverbs 16:5 (TLB), "Pride disgusts the Lord. Take
my word for it—proud men shall be punished."

Punish false witnesses. Track down liars. ...A
false witness shall be punished, and a liar
shall be caught. ...Discipline your son in his
early years while there is hope. If you don't,
you will ruin his life. ...Punish a mocker and
others will learn from his example. Reprove
a wise man, and he will be wiser. Mockers
and rebels shall be severely punished.

Proverbs 19:5, 9, 18, 25, 29 (TLB)

Proverbs 20:22, 26, 30, (TLB) "Don't repay evil for
evil. Wait for the Lord to handle the matter. ...A wise king
stamps out crime by severe punishment. ...Punishment
that hurts chases evil from the heart."

Proverbs 21:11, 15 (TLB), "The wise man learns by listening; the simpleton can only learn by seeing scorners punished. ...A good man loves justice, but it is a calamity to evildoers."

> A prudent man foresees the difficulties
> ahead and prepares for them; the simpleton
> goes blindly on and suffers the consequenc-
> es. ...Teach a child to choose the right path,
> and when he is older, he will remain upon it.
> ...A youngster's heart is filled with rebellion,
> but punishment will drive it out of him. ...
> Don't rob the poor and sick! For the Lord
> is their defender. If you injure them, he will
> punish you.
>
> **Proverbs 22:3, 6, 15, 22–23 (TLB)**

> Don't fail to correct your children; discipline
> won't hurt them! They won't die if you use a
> stick on them! Punishment will keep them
> out of hell. ...O my son, trust my advice—
> stay away from prostitutes. For a prostitute is
> a deep and narrow grave.
>
> **Proverbs 23:13–14, 26 (TLB)**

Any enterprise is built by wise planning,
becomes strong through common sense, and
profits wonderfully by keeping abreast of
the facts. ...You are a poor specimen if you
can't stand the pressure of adversity. ...Do
not rejoice when your enemy meets trouble.
Let there be no gladness when he falls—for
the Lord may be displeased with you and
stop punishing him! ...My son, watch your
step before the Lord and the king, and don't
associate with radicals. For you will go down
with them to sudden disaster, and who
knows where it all will end? ...Develop your
business first before building your house.

Proverbs 24:3–4, 10, 17–18, 21–22, 27 (TLB)

Proverbs 26:3 (TLB), "Guide a horse with a whip, a
donkey with a bridle, and a rebel with a rod to his back!"

Proverbs 27:5–6, 9 (TLB), "Open rebuke is better than
hidden love! Wounds from a friend are better than kisses
from an enemy! ...Friendly suggestions are as pleasant as
perfume."

Scolding and spanking a child helps him to
learn. Left to himself, he brings shame to his
mother. ...Discipline your son and he will

give you happiness and peace of mind. ...
Sometimes mere words are not enough—discipline is needed. For the words may not be heeded. ...Do you want justice? Don't fawn on the judge, but ask the Lord for it!

Proverbs 29:15, 17, 19, 26 (TLB)

Chapter 20:
Gossip

Gossip is thinly veiled information about another that is intended to devalue another's self-worth. Gossip is cowardly because it always hides behind, "I'm just telling you what I heard." The intent of gossip is to tear down or destroy another's reputation, character, and integrity. It always assumes that the person telling the gossip is living on a higher moral plane.

Gossip can flourish in the family, school, church, workplace, and politics. Gossip is very divisive and often embellishes rumors as they cowardly hide behind the thin veil of information and "I thought you ought to know." Gossips often form a self-protective clique that evaluates outsiders' flawed behavior while excusing their own shortcomings.

Stay away from gossip and don't associate with them; otherwise, you may be the next subject of their vile talk.

Proverbs 11:13 (TLB), "A gossip goes around spreading rumors, while a trustworthy man tries to quiet them."

Proverbs 18:8, 21 (TLB), "What dainty morsels rumors are. They are eaten with great relish! …Those who love to talk will suffer the consequences. Men have died for saying the wrong thing!"

Proverbs 20:19 (TLB), "Don't tell your secrets to a gossip unless you want them broadcast to the world."

Proverbs 21:23 (TLB), "Keep your mouth closed and you'll stay out of trouble."

> Telling lies about someone is as harmful as
> hitting him with an axe, or wounding him
> with a sword, or shooting him with a sharp
> arrow. Putting confidence in an unreliable
> man is like chewing with a sore tooth, or
> trying to run on a broken foot.
>
> **Proverbs 25:18–19 (TLB)**

> Fire goes out for lack of fuel, and tensions
> disappear when gossip stops. A quarrelsome
> man starts fights as easily as a match sets
> fire to paper. Gossip is a dainty morsel eaten
> with great relish.
>
> **Proverbs 26:20–22 (TLB)**

Chapter 21:
Hard Work

We have two separate work tasks in life. First, we must work in order to provide food, shelter, and clothing. This has been true since God's curse upon Adam and Eve and all mankind because they disobeyed God and were expelled from the Garden of Eden. The other work task is to work for God in furtherance of His kingdom where our pay doesn't come in the form of money but in eternal rewards.

God, in his kindness, has taught me how to be an expert builder. I have laid the foundation and Apollos has built on it. But he who builds on the foundation must be very careful. And no one can ever lay any other real foundation than that one we already have—Jesus Christ. But there are various kinds of materials that can be used to build on that foundation. Some use gold and silver and jewels; and some build with sticks and hay or even straw! There is going to come a time of testing at Christ's Judgment Day to see what kind of material each builder has used. Everyone's work will be put through the fire so that all can see whether or not it keeps its value, and what was really accomplished. Then every workman who has built on the foundation [Jesus Christ] with the right materials, and whose work still stands, will get his pay. But if the house he has built burns up, he will have a great loss. He himself will be saved, but like a man escaping through a wall of flames.

1 Corinthians 3:10–15 (TLB)

Paul also writes to the Thessalonians that we are to work, stressing that "He who does not work shall not eat" (2 Thessalonians 3:10, TLB). We need to keep our labor for sustenance in balance with our labor for eternal rewards. We can do this because it is God who helps us accomplish His tasks.

Philippians 2:13 (TLB) states, "For God is at work within you, helping you want to obey him, and then helping you do what he wants."

Our work for sustenance must be consistent with our labor for God. Both are to be honorable and performed with integrity.

Proverbs 10:4 (TLB), "Lazy men are soon poor; hard workers get rich."

It is better to get your hands dirty—and eat,
than to be too proud to work—and starve.
…Hard work means prosperity; only a fool
idles away his time. …Telling the truth gives
a man great satisfaction, and hard work
returns many blessings to him. …Work
hard and become a leader; be lazy and never
succeed.

Proverbs 12:9, 11, 14, 24 (TLB)

Proverbs 13:4, 11 (TLB), "Lazy people want much but get little, while the diligent are prospering. …Wealth from gambling quickly disappears; wealth from hard work grows."

The wise man looks ahead. The fool attempts
to fool himself and won't face facts. …The
work of the wicked will perish; the work of
the godly will flourish. …Work brings profit;
talk brings poverty!

Proverbs 14:8, 11, 23 (TLB)

Proverbs 15:22 (TLB), "Plans go wrong with too few counselors; many counselors bring success."

Proverbs 16:1, 3, 26 (TLB), "We can make our plans, but the final outcome is in God's hands. …Commit your work to the Lord, then it will succeed. …Hunger is good—

if it makes you work to satisfy it!"

Proverbs 20:13 (TLB), "If you love sleep, you will end in poverty. Stay awake, work hard, and there will be plenty to eat!"

Proverbs 21:5 (TLB), "Steady plodding brings prosperity; hasty speculation brings poverty."

Proverbs 24:27 (TLB), "Develop your business first before building your house."

Proverbs 25:13 (TLB), "A faithful employee is as refreshing as a cool day in the hot summertime."

Proverbs 26:10 (TLB), "The master may get better work from an untrained apprentice than from a skilled rebel!"

> A workman may eat from the orchard he
> tends; anyone should be rewarded who pro-
> tects another's interests. Riches can disappear
> fast. And the king's crown doesn't stay in
> his family forever—so watch your business
> interest closely.
>
> **Proverbs 27:18, 23–24 (TLB)**

Proverbs 28:12, 19 (TLB), "When the godly are successful, everyone is glad. When the wicked succeed, everyone is sad …Hard work brings prosperity; playing around brings poverty."

Chapter 22:
Honesty (Truth Vs. Lies)

Proverbs 6:16–19 (TLB), "For there are six things the Lord hates—no, seven: haughtiness, lying, murdering, plotting evil, eagerness to do wrong, a false witness, sowing discord among brothers."

Do you realize just how destructive a lie can be to yourself and to someone else? A lie will destroy your integrity and reputation and possibly cause irreparable harm to another. We all must be careful of our speech to ensure that we do not exaggerate or embellish information and certainly do not lie.

> But you are not like that, for the Holy Spirit
> has come upon you, and you know the truth.
> So I am not writing to you as to those who
> need to know the truth, but I warn you as
> those who can discern the difference be-
> tween true and false. And who is the great-
> est liar? The one who says that Jesus is not
> Christ. Such a person is antichrist, for he
> does not believe in God the Father and in
> the Son. For a person who doesn't believe in
> Christ, God's Son, can't have God the Father

either. But he who has Christ, God's Son, has God the Father also.

1 John 2:20–23 (TLB)

By being honest, we are upholding God's truth. When we speak a lie, we are promoting "Satan's lie" and progressing down his pathway.

Certainly, honesty is its own defense. Charles Stanley reminds us that we are to "obey God and leave all the consequences to him."

> Lies will get any man into trouble, but honesty is its own defense. Telling the truth gives a man great satisfaction, and hard work returns many blessings to him. …A good man is known by his truthfulness; a false man by deceit and lies. …Truth stands the test of time; lies are soon exposed. …God delights in those who keep their promises and abhors those who don't [keep their promises].
>
> **Proverbs 12:13–14, 17, 19, 22 (TLB)**

Proverbs 13:5 (TLB), "A good man hates lies; wicked men lie constantly and come to shame."

Proverbs 14:5, 25 (TLB), "A truthful witness never lies; a false witness always lies. …A witness who tells the truth saves good men from being sentenced to death, but a false witness is a traitor."

> The Lord hates the thoughts of the wicked but delights in kind words. Dishonest money brings grief to all the family, but hating bribes brings happiness. A good man thinks before he speaks; the evil man pours out his evil words without a thought.
>
> **Proverbs 15:26–28 (TLB)**

> We can always "prove" that we are right, but is the Lord convinced? …Iniquity is atoned for by mercy and truth; evil is avoided by reverence for God. …A little gained honestly is better than great wealth gotten by dishonest means. …The Lord demands fairness in every business deal. He established this principle. It is a horrible thing for a king [leader] to do evil. His right to rule depends upon his fairness. The king [leader] rejoices when his people are truthful and fair. … The path of the godly leads away from evil; he who follows that path is safe. …An evil man sows strife; gossip separates the best of friends. Wickedness loves company—and leads others into sin [loss].
>
> **Proverbs 16:2, 6, 8, 11–13, 17, 28–29 (TLB)**

The wicked enjoy fellowship with others who are wicked; liars enjoy liars. ...Truth from a rebel or lies from a king [leader] are both unexpected. ...Love forgets mistakes; nagging about them parts the best of friends. ... The Lord despises those who say that bad is good and good is bad.

Proverbs 17:4, 7, 9, 15 (TLB)

The selfish man quarrels against every sound principle of conduct by demanding his own way. A rebel doesn't care about facts. All he wants to do is yell. ...It is wrong for a judge to favor the wicked and condemn the innocent. ...Pride ends in destruction; humility ends in honor.

Proverbs 18:1-2, 5, 12 (TLB)

Proverbs 19:5 (TLB), "Punish false witnesses. Track down liars."

Proverbs 19:9, 22 (KJV): "A false witness shall not be unpunished, and he that speaketh lies shall perish. ...The desire of a man is his kindness: and a poor man is better than a liar."

A king [leader] sitting as judge weighs all
the evidence carefully, distinguishing the
true from false. …The Lord despises every
kind of cheating. …"Utterly worthless!" says
the buyer as he haggles over the price. But
afterwards he brags about his bargain! …
Some men enjoy cheating, but the cake they
buy with such ill-gotten gain will turn to
gravel in their mouths. …The Lord loathes
all cheating and dishonesty. If a king [leader]
is kind, honest, and fair, his kingdom stands
secure.

Proverbs 20:8, 10, 14, 17, 23, 28 (TLB)

We can justify our every deed, but God looks
at our motives. God is more pleased when
we are just and fair than when we give him
gifts. …Dishonest gain will never last, so
why take the risk? …The man who tries to be
good, loving, and kind finds life, righteousness, and honor. …God loathes the gifts of
evil men, especially if they are trying to bribe
him! No one believes a liar, but everyone
respects the words of an honest man.

Proverbs 21:2-3, 6, 21, 27-28 (TLB)

If you must choose, take a good name rather
than great riches; for to be held in loving
esteem is better than silver and gold. ...True
humility and respect for the Lord lead a man
to riches, honor, and long life. ...He who
values grace and truth is the king's [leader's]
friend. ...In the past, haven't I been right?
Then believe what I am telling you now
and share it with others. ...Do you know a
hard-working man? He shall be successful
and stand before kings!

Proverbs 22:1, 4, 11, 20–21, 29 (TLB)

Don't let the sparkle and the smooth taste
of strong wine deceive you. For in the end it
bites like a poisonous serpent; it stings like
an adder. You will see hallucinations and
have delirium tremens, and you will say foolish, silly things that would embarrass you no
end when sober.

Proverbs 23:31–33 (TLB)

Don't envy godless men; don't even enjoy
their company. For they spend their days
plotting violence and cheating. ...Rescue
those who are unjustly sentenced to death;
don't stand back and let them die. Don't

try to disclaim responsibility by saying you didn't know about it. For God, who knows all hearts, knows yours, and he knows you knew! And he will reward everyone according to his deeds. ...Do not rejoice when your enemy meets trouble. Let there be no gladness when he falls. ...He that saith unto the wicked, Thou art righteous; him shall the people curse, nations shall abhor him. ...It is an honor to receive a frank reply. ...Don't testify spitefully against an innocent neighbor. Why lie about him? Don't say, "Now I can pay him back for all his meanness to me!"

Proverbs 24:1–2, 11–12, 17, 26, 28–29 (TLB),

Proverbs 24:24 (KJV)

It is a badge of honor to accept valid criticism. ...Telling lies about someone is as harmful as hitting him with an axe, or wounding him with a sword, or shooting him [with a gun] with a sharp arrow.

Proverbs 25:12, 18 (TLB)

Honor doesn't go with fools anymore than snow with summertime or rain with harvesttime! ...A man who is caught lying to

161

his neighbor and says, "I was just fooling," is like a madman [firing a weapon indiscriminately] throwing around firebrands, arrows, and death. …A man with hate in his heart may sound pleasant enough, but don't believe him; for he is cursing you in his heart. Though he pretends to be so kind, his hatred will finally come to light for all to see. …Flattery is a form of hatred and wounds cruelly.

Proverbs 26:1, 18–19, 24–26, 28 (TLB)

Open rebuke is better than hidden love! Wounds from a friend are better than kisses from an enemy! …Friendly suggestions are as pleasant as perfume. …The purity of silver and gold can be tested in a crucible, but a man is tested by his reaction to men's praise.

Proverbs 27:5–6, 9, 21 (TLB)

Proverbs 28:23–24 (TLB), "In the end, people appreciate frankness more than flattery. A man who robs his parents and says, 'What's wrong with that?' is no better than a murderer."

Proverbs 29:23, 26 (TLB), "Pride ends in a fall, while humility brings honor. …Do you want justice? Don't fawn on the judge, but ask the Lord for it!"

Honesty (Truth Vs. Lies)

O God, I beg two favors from you before I
die: First, help me never to tell a lie. Second,
give me neither poverty nor riches! Give me
just enough to satisfy my needs! …Never
falsely accuse a man to his employer, lest he
curse you for your sin.

Proverbs 30:7–8, 10 (TLB)

Chapter 23:
Joy and Sadness

Psalm 97:10–11 (TLB), "The Lord loves those who hate evil; he protects the lives of his people and rescues them from the wicked. Light is sown for the godly and joy for the good."

Love and joy are inseparable in that, when we love God and love others, we receive joy, peace, patience, kindness, goodness, faithfulness, gentleness, and self-control. These are the (traits) fruit of God's Holy Spirit and are representative of our own tree of life that we share with others.

Christ said, "I have told you this so that my joy may be in you and that your joy may be complete. My command is this: Love each other as I have loved you" (John 15:11–12, NIV).

Proverbs 12:20 (TLB), "Deceit fills hearts that are plotting for evil; joy fills hearts that are planning for good!"

Proverbs 13:13 (TLB), "Despise God's Word and find yourself in trouble. Obey it and succeed."

Proverbs 14:10, 13 (TLB), "Only the person involved can know his own bitterness or joy— no one else can really share it. ...Laughter cannot mask a heavy heart. When the laughter ends, the grief remains."

A wise teacher makes learning a joy; a rebellious teacher spouts foolishness. …A happy face means a glad heart; a sad face means a breaking heart. …When a man is gloomy, everything seems to go wrong; when he is cheerful, everything seems right! … It is better to eat soup with someone you love than steak with someone you hate. …A sensible son gladdens his father. A rebellious son saddens his mother. …The road of the godly leads upward, leaving hell behind. … The Lord hates the thoughts of the wicked but delights in kind words. Dishonest money brings grief to all the family, but hating bribes brings happiness. …Pleasant sights and good reports give happiness and health.

Proverbs 15:2, 13, 15, 17, 20, 24, 26–27, 30 (TLB)

The king [leader] rejoices when his people are truthful and fair. …God blesses those who obey him; happy the man who puts his trust in the Lord. …Kind words are like honey—enjoyable and healthful.

Proverbs 16:13, 20, 24 (TLB)

A dry crust eaten in peace is better than
steak every day along with argument and
strife. ...An old man's grandchildren are his
crowning glory. A child's glory is his father.
...A cheerful heart does good like medicine,
but a broken spirit makes one sick.

Proverbs 17:1, 6, 22 (TLB)

Proverbs 18:20 (TLB), "Ability to give wise advice
satisfies like a good meal!"

Proverbs 19:12 (TLB), "The king's [leader's] anger is
as dangerous as a lion's. But his approval is as refreshing
as the dew on grass."

Proverbs 20:29 (TLB), "The glory of young men is
their strength; of old men, their experience."

It is better to live in the corner of an attic
than with a crabby woman in a lovely home.
...Better to live in the desert than with a
quarrelsome, complaining woman. ...He
[the lazy man] is greedy to get, while the
godly love to give!

Proverbs 21:9, 19, 26 (TLB)

My son, how I will rejoice if you become a
man of common sense. Yes, my heart will
thrill to your thoughtful, wise words. ...The

father of a godly man has cause for joy—
what pleasure a wise son is! So give your
parents joy!

Proverbs 23:15–16, 24–25 (TLB)

When you enjoy becoming wise, there is
hope for you! A bright future lies ahead! …
Do not rejoice when your enemy meets trouble. Let there be no gladness when he falls—
for the Lord may be displeased with you
and stop punishing him! …It is an honor to
receive a frank reply.

Proverbs 24:14, 17–18, 26 (TLB)

Proverbs 25:20 (TLB), "Being happy-go-lucky around
a person whose heart is heavy is as bad as stealing his jack-
et in cold weather or rubbing salt in his wounds."

Proverbs 27:9, 11 (TLB), "Friendly suggestions are as
pleasant as perfume. …My son, how happy I will be if you
turn out to be sensible! It will be a public honor to me."

With good men in authority, the people
rejoice; but with the wicked in power, they
groan. A wise son makes his father happy, but a lad who hangs around prostitutes
disgraces him. …Flattery is a trap; evil men

are caught in it, but good men stay away and
sing for joy.

Proverbs 29:2–3, 5–6 (TLB)

Chapter 24:
A Lazy Man

Ecclesiastes 10:18 (TLB), "Laziness lets the roof leak, and soon the rafters begin to rot."

Now here is a command, dear brothers, given in the name of our Lord Jesus Christ by his authority: Stay away from any Christian who spends his days in laziness and does not follow the ideal of hard work we set up for you. For you well know that you ought to follow our example: you never saw us loafing; we never accepted food from anyone without buying it; we worked hard day and night for the money we needed to live on, in order that we would not be a burden to any of you. It wasn't that we didn't have the right to ask you to feed us, but we wanted to show you firsthand how you should work for your living. Even while we were still there with you, we gave you this rule: "He who does not work shall not eat." Yet we hear that some of you are living in laziness, refusing to work, and wasting your time in gossiping. In the name of the Lord Jesus Christ we appeal to

such people—we command them—to quiet
down, get to work, and earn their own living.
And to the rest of you I say, dear brothers,
never be tired of doing right. If anyone refuses
to obey what we say in this letter, notice who
he is and stay away from him, that he may
be ashamed of himself. Don't think of him as
an enemy, but speak to him as you would a
brother who needs to be warned. May the Lord
of peace himself give you his peace no matter
what happens. The Lord be with you all.

2 Thessalonians 3:6–16 (TLB)

Proverbs 10:4–5 (TLB), "Lazy men are soon poor;
hard workers get rich. A wise youth makes hay while the
sun shines, but what a shame to see a lad who sleeps away
his hour of opportunity."

It is better to get your hands dirty—and eat,
than to be too proud to work—and starve.
…Hard work means prosperity; only a fool
idles away his time. …Work hard and become a leader; be lazy and never succeed.
…A lazy man won't even dress the game
he gets while hunting, but the diligent man
makes good use of everything he finds.

Proverbs 12:9, 11, 24, 27 (TLB)

Proverbs 13:4 (TLB), "Lazy people want much but get little; while the diligent are prospering."

Proverbs 14:4, 23 (TLB), "An empty stable stays clean—but there is no income from an empty stable. ... Work brings profit; talk brings poverty!"

Proverbs 15:19 (TLB), "A lazy fellow has trouble all through life; the good man's path is easy!"

Proverbs 16:27 (TLB), "Idle hands are the devil's workshop; idle lips are his mouthpiece."

Proverbs 18:9 (TLB), "A lazy man is brother to the saboteur."

Proverbs 19:15, 24 (TLB), "A lazy man sleeps soundly—and he goes hungry! ...Some men are so lazy they won't even feed themselves!"

Proverbs 20:4, 13 (TLB), "If you won't plow in the cold, you won't eat at the harvest. ...If you love sleep, you will end in poverty. Stay awake, work hard, and there will be plenty to eat!"

Proverbs 21:25–25 (TLB), "The lazy man longs for many things, but his hands refuse to work. He is greedy to get, while the godly love to give!"

Proverbs 22:13 (TLB), "The lazy man is full of excuses. 'I can't go to work!' he says, 'If I go outside, I might meet a lion in the street and be killed!' [I might be in a car wreck and be killed.]"

Proverbs 23:21 (KJV), "For the drunkard and the glutton shall come to poverty: and a drowsiness shall clothe a man with rags."

Proverbs 24:30–31 (TLB), "I walked by the field of a certain lazy fellow and saw that it was overgrown with thorns; it was covered with weeds, and its walls were broken down."

Proverbs 26:13 (TLB), "The lazy man won't go out and work. 'There might be a lion outside!' he says."

Chapter 25:
Leadership

If you are a preacher, see to it that your sermons are strong and helpful. If God has given you money, be generous in helping others with it. If God has given you administrative ability and put you in charge of the work of others, take the responsibility seriously. Those who offer comfort to the sorrowing should do so with Christian cheer.

Romans 12:8 (TLB)

Leadership knows how to organize, sell, staff, direct, control, produce, market, and evaluate a given product within budgetary constraints in order to meet an objective, usually profit. Leadership requires product knowledge, not only your product but your competition's product as well. The potential pitfalls in any business are always lurking and poised to derail the objective. Leadership will require knowledge of laws and regulations regarding your industry and personnel. Often material shortages, equipment breakdowns, delivery problems, illness, workers conflict, and changes in the industry will consume your attention with little time left to meet your objectives.

A good leader will be a problem solver who can visualize alternatives, make a decision, set priorities, evaluate tactical and strategic intelligence and communicate objectives verbally and in writing. A leader might benefit from advanced degrees in law, psychology, sociology, engineering, government, information technology, and administration and have read all of Peter F. Drucker's books on management.

We tend to lose sight of the original objective to provide goods and services to meet a need. Few in leadership could properly identify their greatest asset or the thing most likely to destroy all of their efforts. This is particularly true of a second-generation family business and persons in an elected office. The greatest asset in any endeavor is the people we employ and serve. The thing most likely to destroy our efforts is sin.

Leadership is one of God's gifts of service. A good leader would do well to study the proverbs and follow the path of common sense, wisdom, knowledge, and understanding.

Proverbs 14:35 (TLB), "A king [leader] rejoices in servants [workers] who know what they are doing; he is angry with those who cause trouble."

Proverbs 15:2 (TLB), "A wise teacher makes learning a joy; a rebellious teacher spouts foolishness."

We should make plans—counting on God
to direct us. God will help the king [leader]
to judge the people fairly; there need be no
mistakes. …It is a horrible thing for a king
[leader] to do evil. His right to rule depends
upon his fairness. The king [leader] rejoices
when his people are truthful and fair. The
anger of the king [leader] is a messenger of
death, and a wise man will appease it. Many
favors are showered on those who please the
king [leader]. …Wisdom is a fountain of life
to those possessing it, but a fool's burden is
his folly. From a wise mind comes careful
and persuasive speech. …We toss the coin,
but it is the Lord who controls its decision.

Proverbs 16:9–10, 12–15, 22–23, 33 (TLB)

Proverbs 17:2, 7, "A wise slave [servant] will rule his
master's [boss'] wicked sons and share their estate. Truth
from a rebel or lies from a king [leader] are both unexpected."

A wise man's words express deep streams of
thought. …A gift does wonders; it will bring
you before men of importance! …A coin toss
ends arguments and settles disputes between
powerful opponents.

Proverbs 18:4, 16, 18 (TLB)

Proverbs 19:10, 12 (TLB), "It doesn't seem right for a fool to succeed or for a slave to rule over princes! ...The king's [leader's] anger is as dangerous as a lion's. But his approval is as refreshing as the dew on grass."

> The king's [leader's] fury is like that of a roaring lion; to rouse his anger is to risk your life. ...A king [leader] sitting as judge weighs all the evidence carefully, distinguishing the true from false. ...A wise king [leader] stamps out crime by severe punishment. ... If a king [leader] is kind, honest, and fair, his kingdom stands secure.
>
> **Proverbs 20:2, 8, 26, 28 (TLB)**

> Just as water is turned into irrigation ditches, so the Lord directs the king's [leader's] thoughts. He turns them wherever he wants to. ...Go ahead and prepare for the conflict, but victory comes from God.
>
> **Proverbs 21:1, 31 (TLB)**

Proverbs 22:8, 11 (TLB), "The unjust tyrant will reap disaster, and his reign of terror shall end. ...He who values grace and truth is the king's [leader's] friend."

> Don't demand an audience with the king [leader] as though you were some powerful

prince. It is better to wait for an invitation
rather than to be sent back to the end of the
line, publicly disgraced! ...One who doesn't
give the gift he promised is like a cloud blow-
ing over a desert without dropping any rain.
...Just as it is harmful to eat too much honey,
so also it is bad for men to think about all
the honors they deserve!

Proverbs 25:6–7, 14, 27 (TLB)

Proverbs 26:10 (TLB), "The master [leader] may get better work from an untrained apprentice than from a skilled rebel!"

Proverbs 27:2 (TLB), "Don't praise yourself; let others do it!"

Proverbs 28:16 (TLB), "Only a stupid prince will oppress his people, but a king [leader] will have a long reign if he hates dishonesty and bribes."

With good men in authority, the people
rejoice; but with the wicked in power, they
groan. ...A just king [leader] gives stability
to his nation, but one who demands bribes
destroys it. ...A king [leader] who is fair to
the poor shall have a long reign. ...When
rulers are wicked, their people are too; but
good men will live to see the tyrant's down-

fall. ...Pamper a servant [worker] from childhood, and he will expect you to treat him as a son!

Proverbs 29:2, 4, 14, 16, 21 (TLB)

Chapter 26:
Mocker (Rebel)

Have you observed a person who has so much confidence in themselves that they will not listen to anything you might say to them? They are not satisfied just by ignoring you; they have to call you a name to belittle you in order to elevate their own self-worth. If you have observed such a person, you have just met a rebel. A rebel has refused to listen to his parents, teachers, and even his friends. His arrogance abounds as he follows a path he has laid out for himself. A brick wall is not enough to deter him. He simply knocks it down or, if necessary, goes over, around, or under it as further proof of his self-sufficiency. He will look at you and say, "You didn't think a little wall would stop me, did you?" as he feeds his arrogant behavior.

A rebel doesn't have a long life expectancy because he does not see the wall as a protection from the impending danger that looms on the other side. Rebellion against all manner of authority will also lead to rejecting God's wisdom, and eventually, he will even mock God.

Parents of a rebellious child must change the child's behavior before they have the opportunity to cause harm spiritually, physically, and emotionally to themselves. The rebellious child is generally more intelligent, divisive, and manipulative. They are inventive and daring and sometimes fearless. They have confidence that the knowledge they possess is sufficient to solve the next problem or challenge. Attempting to find more information by researching the subject or listening to others is simply unnecessary. Rebellious behavior is sometimes an effort to mask or cover up the flaw or deficiencies they see in their own life.

The problem is they will not admit the deficiency to themselves or to their parents. It is up to the parents to discover and deal with the child's deficiency. It took Edison a long time to invent the light bulb, and it may take a long time before the light comes on in the mind of a rebellious child. Proverbs can expose a child to God's wisdom and common sense and set them on a pathway of protection that will guide them away from the looming danger on the other side of the wall. Children must be taught that walls are boundaries placed there for their protection and not simply to be conquered.

Proverbs 13:1, 13 (TLB), "A wise youth accepts his father's rebuke; a young mocker doesn't. …Despise God's Word and find yourself in trouble. Obey it and succeed."

> A rebel's foolish talk should prick his own pride! But the wise man's speech is respected. …A mocker never finds the wisdom he

claims he is looking for, yet it comes easily to the man with common sense. ...The common bond of rebels is their guilt. The common bond of godly people is goodwill.

Proverbs 14:3, 6, 9 (TLB)

A wise teacher makes learning a joy; a rebellious teacher spouts foolishness. ...Only the good can give good advice. Rebels can't. ...A mocker stays away from wise men because he hates to be scolded. ...A wise man is hungry for truth, while the mocker feeds on trash. ...A sensible son gladdens his father. A rebellious son saddens his mother.

Proverbs 15:2, 7, 12, 14, 20 (TLB)

Mocking the poor is mocking the God who made them. He will punish those who rejoice at others' misfortunes. ...Truth from a rebel or lies from a king (leader) are both unexpected. ...A rebuke to a man of common sense is more effective than a hundred lashes on the back of a rebel. ...It is senseless to pay tuition to educate a rebel who has no heart for the truth. ...It's no fun to be a rebel's father. ...A rebellious son is a grief to his father and a bitter blow to his mother.

Proverbs 17:5, 7, 10, 16, 21, 25 (TLB)

Proverbs 18:2 (TLB), "A rebel doesn't care about the facts. All he wants to do is yell [express his opinion]."

Punish a mocker and others will learn from
his example. Reprove a wise man, and he will
be the wiser. A son who mistreats his father
or mother is a public disgrace. ...Mockers
and rebels shall be severely punished.

Proverbs 19:25–26, 29 (TLB)

Proverbs 21:4, 24 (TLB), "Pride, lust, and evil actions are all sin. Mockers are proud, haughty, and arrogant."

The rebel walks a thorny, treacherous road;
the man who values his soul will stay away.
...Throw out the mocker, and you will be
rid of tension, fighting, and quarrels. ...A
youngster's heart is filled with rebellion, but
punishment will drive it out of him.

Proverbs 22:5, 10, 15 (TLB)

Proverbs 24:7, 9 (TLB), "Wisdom is too much for a rebel. He'll not be chosen as a counselor! The rebel's schemes are sinful, and the mocker is the scourge of all mankind."

Putting confidence in an unreliable man is
like chewing on a sore tooth, or trying to run
on a broken foot. A man without self-control
is as defenseless as a city with broken-down
walls [borders].

Proverbs 25:19, 28 (TLB)

Guide a horse with a whip, a donkey with
a bridle, and a rebel with a rod to his back!
…To trust a rebel to convey a message is as
foolish as cutting off your feet and drinking
poison! …Honoring a rebel will backfire
like a stone tied to a slingshot! A rebel will
misapply an illustration so that its point will
no more be felt than a thorn in the hand of a
drunkard. The master [leader] may get better
work from an untrained apprentice than a
skilled rebel!

Proverbs 26:3, 6, 8–10 (TLB)

Proverbs 27:3, 22 (TLB), "A rebel's frustrations are heavier than sand and rocks. You can't separate a rebel from his foolishness though you crush him to powder."

Proverbs 28:7, 9 (TLB), "Young men who are wise obey the law; a son who is a member of a lawless gang is a shame to his father. …God doesn't listen to the prayers of those who flout the law."

Proverbs 29:11 (TLB), "A rebel shouts in anger; a wise man holds his temper in and cools it."

Chapter 27:
The Poor

The book of Proverbs makes it clear that Christians have a responsibility to care for the poor. Moreover, it appears that those who would care for the needs of the poor will have their reward in heaven. Our natural inclination is to befriend the rich, bestow honors on them, invite them to dinners, and shower them with gifts. The ultimate purpose, more often than not, would be the pride you would receive by being a friend to the important person and the recognition you might enjoy.

Although Jesus said that the poor would always be with us, He did not take away our responsibility to care for their needs. When we do, we show the love of God and our obedience to His command.

The first responsibility to care for the poor would appear to fall on the immediate family. Parents should care for the needs of their children. Children should care for elderly parents. Siblings should care for siblings.

The next responsibility would fall on the church to care for the needs of the church family. And each Christian should give generously to the needs of the poor. We should follow Jesus' direction in Luke 14:12–14 (TLB),

Then he turned to the host, "When you put on a dinner," he said, "don't invite friends, brothers, relatives, and rich neighbors! For they will return the invitation. Instead, invite the poor, the crippled, the lame, and the blind. Then at the resurrection of the godly, God will reward you for inviting those who can't repay you."

James 2:5 (TLB), "God has chosen poor people to be rich in faith, and the Kingdom of Heaven is theirs, for that is the gift God has promised to all who love him."

Proverbs 10:15 (TLB), "The rich man's wealth is his only strength. The poor man's poverty is his only curse."

Some rich people are poor, and some poor people have great wealth! …If you refuse criticism, you will end in poverty and disgrace; if you accept criticism, you are on the road to fame. …A poor man's farm may have good soil, but injustice robs him of its riches.

Proverbs 13:7, 18, 23 (TLB)

Even his own neighbors despise the poor man, while the rich have many "friends." But to despise the poor is to sin. Blessed are those who help them. ...Anyone who oppresses the poor is insulting God who made them. To help the poor is to honor God.

Proverbs 14:20–21, 31 (TLB)

Proverbs 15:16, 25 (TLB), "Better a little with reverence for God than great treasure and trouble with it. ...The Lord destroys the possessions of the proud but cares for widows."

Proverbs 16:19 (TLB), "Better poor and humble than proud and rich."

Proverbs 17:5 (TLB), "Mocking the poor is mocking God who made them. He will punish those who rejoice at others' misfortunes."

Proverbs 18:23 (TLB), "The poor man pleads, and the rich man answers with insults."

Better be poor and honest than rich and dishonest. ...A wealthy man has many "friends"; the poor has none left. ...A poor man's own brothers turn away from him in embarrassment; how much more his friends! He calls after them, but they are gone. ...When you help the poor you are lending to the Lord— and he pays wonderful interest on your loan! ...Kindness makes a man attractive. And it is better to be poor than dishonest.

Proverbs 19:1, 4, 7, 17, 22 (TLB)

Steady plodding brings prosperity; hasty speculation brings poverty. ...He who shuts his ears to the cries of the poor will be ignored in his own time of need. ...A man who loves pleasure becomes poor; wine and luxury are not the way to riches!

Proverbs 21:5, 13, 17 (TLB)

The rich and poor are alike before the Lord who made them all. ...Just as the rich rule the poor, so the borrower is servant to the lender. ...Happy is the generous man, the one who feeds the poor. ...He who gains by oppressing the poor or by bribing the rich shall end in poverty. ...Don't rob the poor and sick! For the Lord is their defender. If you injure them, he will punish you.

Proverbs 22:2, 7, 9, 16, 22–23 (TLB)

Don't steal the land of defenseless orphans by moving their ancient boundary marks, for their Redeemer is strong; he himself will accuse you. ...O my son, be wise and stay in

God's paths; don't carouse with drunkards
and gluttons, for they are on their way to
poverty. And remember that too much sleep
clothes a man with rags.

Proverbs 23:10–11, 19–21 (TLB)

Then, as I looked, I learned this lesson: "A
little extra sleep, A little extra slumber, A
little folding of the hands to rest" means that
poverty will break in upon you suddenly like
a robber and violently like a bandit.

Proverbs 24:32–34 (TLB)

When a poor man oppresses those even
poorer, he is like an unexpected flood sweep-
ing away their last hope. ...Better to be poor
and honest than rich and a cheater. ...In-
come from exploiting the poor will end up
in the hands of someone who pities them.
...Rich men are conceited, but their real
poverty is evident to the poor. ...A wicked
ruler is as dangerous to the poor as a lion or
bear attacking them. ...Hard work brings
prosperity; playing around brings poverty.
...Giving preferred treatment to rich people

is a clear case of selling one's soul for a piece of bread. Trying to get rich quick is evil and leads to poverty.

Proverbs 28:3, 6, 8, 11, 15, 19, 21–22 (TLB)

Chapter 28:
The Proud

Brothers, if someone is caught in sin, you
who are spiritual should restore him gen-
tly. But watch yourself, or you also may be
tempted. Carry each other's burdens, and
in this way you will fulfill the law of Christ.
If anyone thinks he is something when he
is nothing, he deceives himself. Each one
should test his own actions. Then he can take
pride in himself, without comparing himself
to someone else, for each one should carry
his own load.

Galatians 6:1–5 (NIV)

We should not think of ourselves more highly than
others. To be boastful, arrogant, and haughty, comparing
yourself to someone who has flaws and failures, will make
you guilty of the greater sin in God's sight. And God said
He would bring your works and efforts to destruction.
God sees into our hearts and knows our thoughts and desires. He will judge our success and failure by the truth
of His Word. All of our accomplishments will be rightful-
ly evaluated and judged according to the talents and gifts

He has provided to each of us. The very accomplishment that brings you the most pride may be destroyed, and what you consider to be a failure might bring you the greatest reward in God's sight. Remember, there are others comparing themselves to you and many who may desire to see your pride suddenly implode in failure.

God desires to do a good work in you. Humble yourself, study to show your desire to do His will, and He will crown your efforts with success. Solomon, in his desire to please God, was given an abundant reward.

Proverbs 11:2, 22 (TLB), "Proud men end in shame, but the meek become wise. ...A beautiful woman lacking discretion and modesty is like a fine gold ring in a pig's snout."

Proverbs 12:9 (TLB), "It is better to get your hands dirty—and eat, than to be too proud to work—and starve."

Proverbs 13:10 (TLB), "Pride leads to arguments; be humble, take advice, and become wise."

Proverbs 14:3 (TLB), "A rebel's foolish talk should prick his own pride! But the wise man's speech is respected."

Proverbs 15:25 (TLB), "The Lord destroys the possessions of the proud but cares for the widows."

Proverbs 16:5, 18–19 (TLB), "Pride disgusts the Lord. Take my word for it—proud men shall be punished. ... Pride goes before destruction and haughtiness before a fall. Better poor and humble than proud and rich."

Proverbs 18:12 (TLB), "Pride ends in destruction; humility ends in honor."

Proverbs 21:4, 24, 30 (TLB), "Pride, lust, and evil actions are all sin. ...Mockers are proud, haughty, and arrogant. ...No one, regardless of how shrewd or well-advised [proud] he is, can stand against the Lord."

> Don't demand an audience with the king as
> though you were some powerful prince. It is
> better to wait for an invitation rather than to
> be sent back to the end of the line, publicly
> disgraced! ...It is a badge of honor to accept
> valid criticism.
>
> **Proverbs 25:6–7, 12 (TLB)**

> Don't brag about your plans for tomorrow—
> wait and see what happens. Don't praise
> yourself; let others do it! The purity of silver
> and gold can be tested in a crucible, but a
> man is tested by his reaction to men's praise.
>
> **Proverbs 27:1–2, 21 (TLB)**

Proverbs 28:26 (TLB), "A man is a fool to trust himself! But those who use God's wisdom are safe."

Chapter 29:
Reverence

How does a man become wise? The first step
is to trust and reverence the Lord! Only fools
refuse to be taught. Listen to your father
and mother. What you learn from them will
stand you in good stead; it will gain you
many honors.

Proverbs 1:7–9 (TLB)

Second Corinthians 7:1 (NIV), "Since we have these
promises, dear friends, let us purify ourselves from everything that contaminates body and spirit, perfecting holiness out of reverence for God."

Reverence and fear of a Holy God is the beginning of
wisdom. Reverence, holiness, and sanctification appear to
be forgotten concepts in our world today. We live in a "me,
me, me" society with little thought of why God has placed
us here for such a time as this. He didn't place us here to
look like and act like everyone else, nor did He want us
to be so different that we draw attention to ourselves. We
should respect and honor a Holy God in appearance and
actions. How we dress in God's house is important. This is
not the place for seductive or sloppy attire, which exposes
portions of our body inappropriately.

Proverbs 11:22 (TLB) says, "A beautiful woman lacking discretion and modesty is like a fine gold ring in a pig's snout." Although rarely mentioned from the pulpit, our appearance is a reflection of our respect for God. It is not necessary to look like the world to attract the world to Christ. If you look like the world and act like the world, just what do you think sets you apart from the world? We, who are a part of God's family, show our respect to a Holy God and reflect Christ in all of our ways.

God desires that we be obedient to His Word, which is truth, and to do His will. He will show you His will if you humble yourself and pray, expecting to receive an answer. When the Holy Spirit abides in you, there is a direct line of communication between you and God. When you pray, look for God's response; it will come to you through His Spirit that is within you. His Spirit is there to give you the wisdom and guidance to accomplish His will as He provides protection and the assurance of eternal life. Christ is coming again. We saw Him as a baby in a manger and helplessly sacrificed on a cross. He was stripped of His robe and crowned in mockery as the king of the Jews. But He was raised from the dead and appeared to the disciples and hundreds more. He is alive and returning as King of kings with many crowns and a brilliant white robe dipped in blood for the whole world to see. He will have all power and authority to rule and reign over Earth. Shouldn't we show honor and reverence to an awesome and Holy God?

Proverbs 10:27 (TLB), "Reverence for God adds hours to each day; so how can the wicked expect a long, good life?"

> Your riches won't help you on Judgment
> Day; only righteousness counts then. ...
> You can be very sure the evil man will not
> go unpunished forever. And you can also be
> very sure God will rescue the children of the
> godly. ...Godly men are growing a tree that
> bears life-giving fruit, and all who win souls
> are wise.
>
> **Proverbs 11:4, 21, 30 (TLB)**

Proverbs 14:26–27 (TLB), "Reverence for God gives a man deep strength; his children have a place of refuge and security. Reverence for the Lord is a fountain of life; its waters keep a man from death."

> Better is little with reverence for God than
> great treasure and trouble with it. ...The
> Lord is far from the wicked, but he hears the
> prayers of the righteous. ...Humility and
> reverence for the Lord will make you both
> wise and honored.
>
> **Proverbs 15:16, 29, 33 (TLB)**

We can make our plans, but the final outcome is in God's hands. ...Iniquity is atoned
for by mercy and truth; evil is avoided by
reverence for God. When a man is trying
to please God, God makes even his worst
enemies to be at peace with him. ...We toss
the coin, but it is the Lord who controls its
decision.

Proverbs 16:1, 6–7, 33 (TLB)

Proverbs 19:23 (TLB), "Reverence for God gives life, happiness, and protection from harm."

Proverbs 21:3 (TLB), "God is more pleased when we are just and fair than when we give him gifts."

Proverbs 22:4 (TLB), "True humility and respect for the Lord lead a man to riches, honor, and a long life."

Evil men don't understand the importance
of justice, but those who follow the Lord are
much concerned about it. ...A man who
refuses to admit his mistakes can never be
successful. But if he confesses and forsakes
them, he gets another chance. Blessed is the
man who reveres God, but the man who
doesn't care is headed for serious trouble.
...The man who wants to do right will get a

rich reward. But the man who wants to get rich quick will quickly fail. ...A man is a fool to trust himself! But those who use God's wisdom are safe.

Proverbs 28:5, 13–14, 20, 26 (TLB)

Proverbs 29:18 (KJV), "Where there is no vision, the people perish: but he that keepeth the law, happy is he."

Proverbs 29:23, 25 (TLB), "Pride ends in a fall, while humility brings honor. ...Fear of man is a dangerous trap, but to trust in God means safety."

Proverbs 29:26 (KJV), "Many seek the ruler's favor; but every man's judgment cometh from the Lord."

Chapter 30:
Rich Man—Wealth

O God, I beg two favors from you before I
die: First, help me never to tell a lie. Second,
give me neither poverty nor riches! Give me
just enough to satisfy my needs! For if I grow
rich, I may become content without God.
And if I am too poor, I may steal and thus
insult God's holy name.

Proverbs 30:7–9 (TLB)

One of life's greatest pursuits is wealth. We spend extra hours each day, each week, or each year trying to get ahead. Just what are we trying to get ahead of?

Maybe it is ahead of where we are now or ahead of our neighbors or coworkers.

Twentieth-century banking has given us a plastic card in order to borrow from the future. What may have been intended as a convenient and safe manner to carry money turned out to be a quick method of borrowing from future earnings. The Bible says, "For a man is a slave to whatever controls him" (2 Peter 2:19, TLB).

If you borrow money, you are allowing yourself to be a slave to someone. Likewise, when a country borrows money, they are allowing its citizens to be slaves to another country.

Pursuing wealth is hardly a worthwhile endeavor, yet some devote almost every waking hour attempting to earn more in order to have more. We fail to realize that with wealth comes hardship and stress. For whatever we own, in reality, owns us. The end result might just be that we are a slave to the things we own.

We can see what the Bible says about this in Ephesians 5:5 (TLB),

> You can be sure of this: the kingdom of
> Christ and of God will never belong to
> anyone who is impure or greedy, for a greedy
> person is really an idol worshipper—he loves
> and worships the good things of this life
> more than God.

Proverbs 10:15, 22 (TLB), "The rich man's wealth is his only strength. The poor man's poverty is his only curse. …The Lord's blessing is our greatest wealth. All our work adds nothing to it!"

> Your riches won't help you on Judgment
> Day; only righteousness counts then. …
> Honor goes to kind and gracious women,
> mere money to cruel men. …The evil man
> gets rich for the moment, but the good man's

reward lasts forever. ...Trust in your money
and down you go! Trust in God and flourish
as a tree!

Proverbs 11:4, 16, 18, 28 (TLB)

Lazy people want much but get little, while
the dili-gent are prospering. ...Some rich
people are poor, and some poor people
have great wealth! ...Wealth from gambling
quickly disappears; wealth from hard work
grows. ...Despise God's Word and find yourself in trouble. Obey it and succeed. ...When
a good man dies, he leaves an inheritance to
his grandchildren; but when a sinner dies,
his wealth is stored up for the godly.

Proverbs 13:4, 7, 11, 13, 22 (TLB)

Proverbs 14:20, 23, "Even his own neighbors despise
the poor man, while the rich have many 'friends.' ...Work
brings profit; talk brings poverty!"

Better a little with reverence for God than
great treasure and trouble with it. ...Plans
go wrong with too few counselors; many
counselors bring success. ...The Lord destroys the possessions of the proud but cares
for widows. ...Dishonest money brings grief

to all the family, but hating bribes brings happiness.

Proverbs 15:16, 22, 25, 27 (TLB)

A little gained honestly is better than great wealth gotten by dishonest means. ...How much better is wisdom than gold, and understanding than silver! ...Better poor and humble than proud and rich.

Proverbs 16:8, 16, 19 (TLB)

Proverbs 17:8, 18 (TLB), "A bribe [gift] works like magic. Whoever uses it will prosper! ...It is poor judgment to countersign another's note, to become responsible for his debts."

Proverbs 18:11, 23 (TLB), "The rich man thinks of his wealth as an impregnable defense, a high wall of safety. What a dreamer! ...The poor man pleads, and the rich man answers with insults."

Better be poor and honest than rich and dishonest. ...A wealthy man has many "friends"; the poor man has none left [friends]. ...Many beg favors from a man who is generous; everyone is his friend! ...A father can give his sons homes and riches, but only the Lord can give them understanding wives. ...When you help the poor you are lending to the Lord— and he pays wonderful interest on your loan!

Proverbs 19:1, 4, 6, 14, 17 (TLB)

Proverbs 20:15 (TLB), "Good sense is far more valuable than gold or precious jewels [wealth]."

Proverbs 21:5, 17 (TLB), "Steady plodding brings prosperity; hasty speculation brings poverty. ...A man who loves pleasure becomes poor; wine and luxury are not the way to riches!"

If you must choose, take a good name rather than great riches; for to be held in loving esteem is better than silver and gold. The rich and poor are alike before the Lord who made them all. ...True humility and respect for the Lord lead a man to riches, honor, and long life. ...Just as the rich rule the poor, so the borrower is servant to the lender. ...He who gains by oppressing the poor or by bribing the rich shall end in poverty. ...Don't rob the poor and sick! For the Lord is their defender. If you injure them, he will punish you.

Proverbs 22:1–2, 4, 7, 16, 22–23 (TLB)

When dining with a rich man [ruler], be on
your guard and don't stuff yourself, though
it all tastes so good; for he is trying to bribe
you, and no good is going to come of his
invitation. Don't weary yourself trying to get
rich. Why waste your time? For riches can
disappear as though they had the wings of a
bird!

Proverbs 23:1–5 (TLB)

Any enterprise is built by wise planning,
becomes strong through common sense, and
profits wonderfully by keeping abreast of the
facts. …Develop your business first before
building your house.

Proverbs 24:3–4, 27 (TLB)

Proverbs 27:23–24 (TLB), "Riches can disappear fast.
And the king's crown doesn't stay in his family forever—
so watch your business interests closely."

Better to be poor and honest than rich and a
cheater. …Rich men are conceited, but their
real poverty is evident to the poor. When
the godly are successful, everyone is glad.
When the wicked succeed, everyone is sad.
…The man who wants to do right will get a

rich reward. But the man who wants to get rich quick will quickly fail. Giving preferred treatment to rich people is a clear case of selling one's soul for a piece of bread. Trying to get rich quick is evil and leads to poverty. ...Greed causes fighting; trusting God leads to prosperity. ...When the wicked prosper, good men go away; when the wicked meet disaster, good men return.

Proverbs 28:6, 11–12, 20–22, 25, 28 (TLB)

Proverbs 29:13 (TLB), "Rich and poor are alike in this: each depends on God for light."

Chapter 31:
Sadness–Breaking Heart

Ecclesiastes 12:1 (NIV), "Remember your Creator in the days of your youth, before the days of trouble come and the years approach when you will say, 'I find no pleasure in them.'"

Seek wisdom while you are young in order that you live a long life with the fear and knowledge of God to guide and protect you.

You will find sadness if your life's pursuit is for wealth and suddenly misfortune takes it away. You may discover that your wealth has made it possible to obtain property and possessions which are too burdensome to maintain. Or you may realize that failing health and the brevity of this life have placed a greater priority on the intangible things of life.

Realize that when sadness comes, it is time to pause and remember the times of joy and gladness and trust God to cause all things to happen for our good.

Wisdom will protect you from the snares and pitfalls of "Satan's lie." Listen to your conscience when it tells you to heed the warning signs. It is better to avoid a moment of pleasure than to experience a lifetime of regret.

Ecclesiastes 7:26 (NIV), "I find more bitter than death the woman who is a snare, whose heart is a trap and whose hands are chains. The man who pleases God will escape her, but the sinner she will ensnare."

> Here is my final conclusion: fear God and
> obey his commandments, for this is the
> entire duty of man. For God will judge us for
> everything we do, including every hidden
> thing, good or bad.
>
> **Ecclesiastes 12:13–14 (TLB)**

> A happy face means a glad heart; a sad
> face means a breaking heart. A wise man is
> hungry for truth, while the mocker feeds on
> trash. When a man is gloomy, everything
> seems to go wrong; when he is cheerful,
> everything seems right! Better a little with
> reverence for God than great treasure and
> trouble with it. It is better to eat soup with
> someone you love than steak with someone
> you hate. …Everyone enjoys giving good
> advice, and how wonderful it is to be able to
> say the right thing at the right time.
>
> **Proverbs 15:13–17, 23 (TLB)**

> A dry crust eaten in peace is better than
> steak every day along with argument and
> strife. …It is hard to stop a quarrel once
> it starts, so don't let it begin. …A cheerful
> heart does good like medicine, but a broken
> spirit makes one sick.
>
> **Proverbs 17:1, 14, 22 (TLB)**

Proverbs 18:3, 14 (TLB), "Sin brings disgrace. …A man's courage [spirit] can sustain a broken body, but when courage dies, what hope is left?"

Proverbs 21:9, 19 (TLB), "It is better to live in the corner of an attic than with a crabby woman in a lovely home. …Better to live in the desert than with a quarrelsome, complaining woman."

> One who doesn't give a gift he promised is
> like a cloud blowing over a desert without
> dropping any rain. …Being happy-go-lucky
> around a person whose heart is heavy is as
> bad as stealing his jacket in cold weather or
> rubbing salt in his wounds.
>
> **Proverbs 25:14, 20 (TLB)**

> If you shout a pleasant greeting to a friend
> too early in the morning, he will count it as
> a curse! A constant dripping on a rainy day

and a cranky woman are much alike! You
can no more stop her complaints than you
can stop the wind or hold onto anything
with greasy hands.

Proverbs 27:14–16 (TLB)

Chapter 32:
A Wicked Man (Evil)

If my people, which are called by my name,
shall humble themselves, and pray, and seek
my face, and turn from their wicked ways;
then will I hear from heaven, and will forgive
their sin, and heal their land.

2 Chronicles 7:14 (KJV)

When Solomon completed the building of God's temple, the Lord appeared to him and spoke the above words for the benefit of those who were called by the Lord's name.

The wickedness of this world was as evident in the day of Noah, Solomon, and Christ as it is today. The love of sin appears to increase exponentially with each new generation. The lure of money, power, sexual sin, and all manner of wicked thought has sent many down an evil path so far that they appear unable to hear the message of God's forgiveness.

The evil man spends his time plotting his greed at the expense of others and lays a trap for others. God's Word says that God causes the wicked to fall into their own trap. We should be very careful to recognize the ways of the wicked in order to avoid their trap and their evil ways.

> Having such great promises as these [to be
> sons of God], dear friends, let us turn away
> from everything wrong [evil], whether of
> body or spirit, and purify ourselves, living in
> the wholesome fear of God, giving ourselves
> to him alone.

2 Corinthians 7:1 (TLB)

Satan has laid a trap to capture your soul, and evil persons in this world are there to assist him. He thinks he knows you well enough to know your weakest areas, where you are most vulnerable. We all must listen to the warnings of our conscience and rely on God's Word as an assurance of His protection from Satan's fiery darts.

Stay away from the evil pathway because it has many pitfalls and traps, some of them deadly. You have no control over the consequences of evil apart from the protection of "God's truth." Remember that faith is your shield against evil.

A word of caution may be helpful because some would ignore wisdom and common sense by inviting addicts into their homes and churches. Such programs can be beneficial, but care should be given to protect your home, your church, and your children from the influence of "evil" that can accompany these men. Justice is blind; faith is not. Faith in God is demonstrated by wisdom, common sense, and understanding.

Dr. David Jeremiah, in his book *What in the World Is Going On?* said it well,

> What I say next is not easy for me to say but I think I must say it anyway. One of the nicest things about American people is that you are generous and friendly people, and because of this you are sometimes naive and overly trusting. You want to be friendly, so you open up to people and then you're surprised when they stab you in the back.

Satan wants to gain entry into our homes, churches, and our country. Don't naively open the door and welcome him in.

> The Lord will not let a good man starve to death, nor will he let the wicked man's riches continue forever. ...The good man is covered with blessings from head to foot, but an evil man inwardly curses his luck. We all have happy memories of good men gone to their reward, but the names of wicked men stink after them. ...There is living truth in what

a good man says, but the mouth of the evil man is filled with curses. ...Disaster strikes like a cyclone and the wicked are whirled away. But the good man has a strong anchor. ...Reverence for God adds hours to each day; so how can the wicked expect a long, good life? The hope of good men is eternal happiness; the hopes of evil men are all in vain. God protects the upright but destroys the wicked. ...The upright speak what is helpful; the wicked speak rebellion.

Proverbs 10:3, 6–7, 11, 25, 27–29, 32 (TLB)

Good people are directed by their honesty; the wicked shall fall beneath their load of sins. The good man's goodness delivers him; the evil man's treachery is his undoing. ... God rescues good men from danger while letting the wicked fall into it. ...The whole city celebrates a good man's success—and also the godless man's death. The good influence of godly citizens causes a city to prosper, but the moral decay of the wicked drives it downhill. ...The good man finds life; the evil man, death. ...You can be very sure the evil man will not go unpunished forever. And you can also be very sure God will rescue the children of the godly. ...The good man can look forward to happiness, while the wicked can expect only wrath. ...If you search for good, you will find God's favor; if you search for evil, you will find his curse. ...Even the godly shall be rewarded here on earth; how much more the wicked!

Proverbs 11:5–6, 8, 10–11, 19, 21, 23, 27, 31 (TLB)

The Lord blesses good men and condemns the wicked. Wickedness never brings real success; only the godly have that. ...The wicked accuse; the godly defend. The wicked shall perish; the godly shall stand. Everyone admires a man with good sense, but a man with a warped mind is despised. ...A good man is known by his truthfulness; a false man by deceit and lies. ...Deceit fills hearts that are plotting for evil; joy fills hearts that are planning for good! No real harm befalls the good, but there is constant trouble for the wicked. ...The good man asks advice from friends; the wicked plunge ahead—and fall.

Proverbs 12:2–3, 6–8, 17, 20–21, 26 (TLB)

Proverbs 13:2, 25 (TLB), "The good man wins his case by careful arguments; the evil-minded only wants to fight.

…The good man eats to live, while the evil man lives to eat."

> The work of the wicked will perish; the work
> of the godly will flourish. …Those who plot
> evil shall wander away and be lost, but those
> who plan good shall be granted mercy and
> quietness. …The godly have a refuge when
> they die, but the wicked are crushed by their
> sins.
>
> **Proverbs 14:11, 22, 32 (TLB)**

> There is treasure in being good, but trouble
> dogs the wicked. …The Lord hates the gifts
> of the wicked but delights in the prayers
> of his people. The Lord despises the deeds
> of the wicked but loves those who try to
> be good. …A good man thinks before he
> speaks; the evil man pours out his evil words
> without a thought. The Lord is far from the
> wicked, but he hears the prayers of the righ-
> teous.
>
> **Proverbs 15:6, 8–9, 28–29 (TLB)**

> The Lord has made everything for his own
> purposes—even the wicked for punishment.
> …Wickedness loves company—and leads

others into sin. The wicked man stares into
space with pursed lips, deep in thought,
planning his evil deeds.

Proverbs 16:4, 29–30 (TLB)

The wicked enjoy fellowship with others who
are wicked; liars enjoy liars. …The wicked
live for rebellion; they shall be severely punished. …An evil man is suspicious of everyone and tumbles into constant trouble.

Proverbs 17:4, 11, 20 (TLB)

Proverbs 18:6–7 (TLB), "A fool gets into constant
fights. His mouth is his undoing! His words endanger him."

Pride, lust, and evil actions are all sin. …
Because the wicked are unfair, their violence boomerangs and destroys them. …
An evil man loves to harm others; being a
good neighbor is out of his line. …God, the
Righteous One, knows what is going on in
the homes of the wicked and will bring the
wicked to judgment. …A good man loves
justice, but it is a calamity to evildoers. …
The wicked will finally lose; the righteous
will finally win. …An evil man is stubborn,
but a godly man will reconsider.

Proverbs 21:4, 7, 10, 12, 15, 18, 29 (TLB)

Proverbs 22:12 (TLB), "The Lord preserves the upright but ruins the plans of the wicked."

Proverbs 23:6 (TLB), "Don't associate with evil men; don't long for their favors and gifts. Their kindness is a trick; they want to use you as their pawn."

> Don't envy godless men; don't even enjoy their company. For they spend their days plotting violence and cheating. …To plan evil is as wrong as doing it. …O evil man, leave the upright man alone and quit trying to cheat him out of his rights. Don't you know that this good man, though you trip him up seven times, will each time rise again? But one calamity is enough to lay you low. …Don't envy the wicked. Don't covet his riches. For the evil man has no future; his light will be snuffed out. …He who says to the wicked, "You are innocent," shall be cursed by many people of many nations.
>
> **Proverbs 24:1–2, 8, 15–16, 19–20, 24 (TLB)**

Proverbs 25:26, 28 (TLB), "If a godly man compromises with the wicked, it is like polluting a fountain or muddying a spring. …A man without self-control is as defenseless as a city with broken-down walls."

A man with hate in his heart may sound pleasant enough, but don't believe him; for he is cursing you in his heart. Though he pretends to be so kind, his hatred will finally come to light for all to see.

Proverbs 26:24–26 (TLB)

The wicked flee when no one is chasing them! But the godly are bold as lions! …God doesn't listen to the prayers of those who flout the law. …When the godly are success-ful, everyone is glad. When the wicked suc-ceed, everyone is sad. …A murderer's con-science will drive him into hell. Don't stop him! Good men will be rescued from harm, but cheaters will be destroyed. …When the wicked prosper, good men go away; when the wicked meet disaster, good men return.

Proverbs 28:1, 9, 12, 17–18, 28 (TLB)

The man who is often reproved but refuses to accept criticism will suddenly be broken and never have another chance. With good men in authority, the people rejoice; but with the wicked in power, they groan. …Flattery is a trap; evil men are caught in it, but good men stay away and sing for joy. The good man

knows the poor man's rights; the godless
don't care. …A wicked ruler will have wicked
aides on his staff. …When rulers are wicked, their people are too; but good men will
live to see the tyrant's downfall. …A man
who assists a thief must really hate himself!
For he knows the consequence but does it
anyway. …The good hate the badness of the
wicked. The wicked hate the goodness of the
good.

Proverbs 29:1–2, 5–7, 12, 16, 24, 27 (TLB)

Chapter 33:
The Wise

Proverbs 8:33 (TLB), "Listen to my counsel—oh, don't refuse it—and be wise."

The reverence and fear of the Lord is the beginning of wisdom. Knowing God through Christ leads to every other kind of understanding. Wisdom is standing ready to pour out knowledge and common sense upon anyone who will seek it as they would look for treasure. Wisdom leads to a long life with honor and riches beyond all that you could imagine. Following wisdom's pathway assures peace and eternal security.

Why is it that we do not have classes in wisdom for children? If we know wisdom is foundational to all knowledge and understanding, why is it not taught in public schools and colleges? Moreover, why is it not taught in churches for children and adults?

Is it any wonder that we are in pursuit of answers to the wrong questions? "Satan's lies" have us on the wrong path asking for answers to the wrong questions. Where is wisdom to be found when we are on the wrong path? We now have governments making laws when they either do not know or understand God's laws. Ignorance of God's laws has lawmakers legislating on same-sex marriages, when to abort a fetus, and whether there should be homosexuals in the military. Is there any hope that we can govern the masses when we are so far down the maze of Satan's pathway that it seems impossible to arrive at a reasonable solution?—Mazeltov!

Thanks be to God that we have His Word to guide us to wisdom and understanding. Knowing Christ is our means of retaining hope in the midst of chaos.

> A wise youth makes hay while the sun shines, but what a shame to see a lad who sleeps away his hour of opportunity. …A wise man holds his tongue. Only a fool blurts out everything he knows; that only leads to sorrow and trouble. …A fool's fun is being bad; a wise man's fun is being wise! …The good man gives wise advice, but the liar's counsel is shunned.
>
> **Proverbs 10:5, 14, 23, 31 (TLB)**

Proverbs 11:14, 30 (TLB), "Without wise leadership, a nation is in trouble; but with good counselors there is safety. …Godly men are growing a tree that bears life-giving fruit, and all who win souls are wise."

Proverbs 12:18, 23 (TLB), "Some people like to make cutting remarks, but the words of the wise soothe and heal.

A wise man doesn't display his knowledge, but a fool displays his foolishness."

> A wise youth accepts his father's rebuke; a young mocker doesn't. …Pride leads to arguments; be humble, take advice, and become wise. …The advice of a wise man refreshes like water from a mountain spring. Those accepting it become aware of the pitfalls on ahead. …A wise man thinks ahead; a fool doesn't and even brags about it! …Be with wise men and become wise. Be with evil men and become evil.
>
> **Proverbs 13:1, 10, 14, 16, 20 (TLB)**

> A rebel's foolish talk should prick his own pride! But the wise man's speech is respected. …A wise man is cautious and avoids danger; a fool plunges ahead with great confidence. …The simpleton is crowned with folly; the wise man is crowned with knowledge. …A wise man controls his temper. He knows that anger causes mistakes.
>
> **Proverbs 14:3, 16, 18, 29 (TLB)**

> A wise teacher makes learning a joy; a rebellious teacher spouts foolishness. …Only

a fool despises his father's advice; a wise son considers each suggestion. …A mocker stays away from wise men because he hates to be scolded. …A wise man is hungry for truth, while the mocker feeds on trash. …Plans go wrong with too few counselors; many counselors bring success. Everyone enjoys giving good advice, and how wonderful it is to be able to say the right thing at the right time! …If you profit from constructive criticism, you will be elected to the wise men's hall of fame. But to reject criticism is to harm yourself and your own best interest. Humility and reverence for the Lord will make you both wise and honored.

Proverbs 15:2, 5, 12, 14, 22–23, 31–33 (TLB)

When a man is trying to please God, God makes even his worst enemies to be at peace with him. …We should make plans—counting on God to direct us. …How much better is wisdom than gold, and understanding than silver! The path of the godly leads away from evil; he who follows that path is safe. …God blesses those who obey him; happy the man who puts his trust in the Lord. The wise man is known by his common sense, and a pleasant teacher is the best. Wisdom is a fountain of life to those possessing it, but a fool's burden is his folly. From a wise mind comes careful and persuasive speech. ...It is better to be slow-tempered than famous; it is better to have self-control than to control an army.

Proverbs 16:7, 9, 16–17, 20–23, 32 (TLB)

A wise slave [servant] will rule his master's wicked sons and share their estate. ...The man of few words and settled mind is wise; therefore, even a fool is thought to be wise when he is silent. It pays him to keep his mouth shut.

Proverbs 17:2, 27–28 (TLB)

A wise man's words express deep streams of thought. ...The intelligent man is always open to new ideas. In fact, he looks for them. ...Ability to give wise advice satisfies like a good meal!

Proverbs 18:4, 15, 20 (TLB)

He who loves wisdom loves his own best interest and will be a success. ,...A wise man restrains his anger and overlooks insults.

> This is to his credit. …Keep the command-
> ments and keep your life; despising them
> means death. …Get all the advice you can
> and be wise the rest of your life. …Punish
> a mocker and others will learn from his
> example. Reprove a wise man, and he will be
> the wiser. …Stop listening to teaching that
> contradicts what you know is right.
>
> **Proverbs 19:8, 11, 16, 20, 25, 27**

Proverbs 19:27 (NIV), "Stop listening to instruction, my son, and you will stray from the words of knowledge."

> The wise man learns by listening; the simple-
> ton can learn only by seeing scorners pun-
> ished. …The wise man saves for the future,
> but the foolish man spends whatever he gets.
> …The wise man conquers the strong man
> and levels his defenses.
>
> **Proverbs 21:11, 20, 22 (TLB)**

Proverbs 22:17–19 (TLB), "Listen to this wise advice; follow it closely, for it will do you good, and you can pass it on to others: Trust in the Lord."

> Don't waste your breath on a rebel. He will
> despise the wisest advice. …My son, how
> I will rejoice if you become a man of com-
> mon sense. Yes, my heart will thrill to your

thoughtful, wise words. …O my son, be
wise and stay in God's paths; don't carouse
with drunkards and gluttons, for they are on
their way to poverty. And remember that too
much sleep clothes a man with rags.

Proverbs 23:9, 15–16, 19–21 (TLB)

Any enterprise is built by wise planning,
becomes strong through common sense, and
profits wonderfully by keeping abreast of the
facts. A wise man is mightier than a strong
man. Wisdom is mightier than strength. …
Wisdom is too much for a rebel. He'll not
be chosen as a counselor. …My son, honey
whets the appetite, and so does wisdom!
When you enjoy becoming wise, there is
hope for you! A bright future lies ahead!

Proverbs 24:3–5, 7, 13–14 (TLB)

Proverbs 25:12 (TLB), "It is a badge of honor to accept
valid criticism."

Proverbs 28:7, 26 (TLB), "Young men who are wise
obey the law; a son who is a member of a lawless gang is a
shame to his father. …A man is a fool to trust himself! But
those who use God's wisdom are safe."

A wise son makes his father happy, but a lad who hangs around with prostitutes disgraces him. ...Fools start fights everywhere while wise men try to keep peace. ...The godly pray for those who long to kill them. A rebel shouts in anger; a wise man holds his temper in and cools it.

Proverbs 29:3, 8, 10–11 (TLB)

Conclusion:
Wisdom's Final Plea

I, Wisdom, give good advice and common sense. Because of my strength, kings reign in power, and rulers make just laws. I love all who love me. Those who search for me shall surely find me. Unending riches, honor, justice, and righteousness are mine to distribute. My gifts are better than the purest gold or sterling silver! My paths are those of justice and right. Those who love and follow me are indeed wealthy. I fill their treasuries. The Lord formed me in the beginning, before he created anything else. From ages past, I am. I existed before the earth began. I lived before the oceans were created, before the springs bubbled forth their waters onto the earth, before the mountains and the hills were made. Yes, I was born before God made the earth and fields and the first handfuls of soil. I was there when he established the heavens and formed the great springs in the depths of the oceans. I was there when he set the limits of the seas and gave them his instructions not to spread beyond their boundaries. I was there when he made the blueprint for the earth and oceans. I was the craftsman at his side. I was his constant delight, rejoicing always in his presence. And how happy I was with what he created—his wide world and all his family of mankind! And so, young men, listen to me, for how happy are all who follow my instructions.

Proverbs 8:14–32 (TLB)

Amen and Amen

A Truth—A Truth

A Confession of Faith

The Cross

When you look at the cross, what do you see?

Let me tell you what it means to me.

It's more than just two pieces of wood stuck in the ground

It's where love, faith, and joy can be found

The cross is a symbol of Christ.

It's where Jesus paid the price.

He paid the price for you and me.

So by believing in Him, we are free.

Free from sin, we can be.

His Word says, "Follow Me."

Now that I have told you what it means to me.

When you look at the cross, what do you see?

Jake McConnell
Age twelve

FDA-DEA
Blessed–So Help Me God

By wholly trusting in His Word, God has shown me the paths I should follow and the very steps I should take as He protected and encouraged me. Because of my commitment to following His direction, I have written a book about my experience working for the DEA and its predecessor agencies. I wrote this book to demonstrate how God could use a person with a severe learning disability to accomplish more than I ever dreamed possible.